OECD ECONOMIC SURVEYS

1993-1994

CANADA

ORGANISATION FOR ECONOMIC CO-OPERATION AND DEVELOPMENT

ORGANISATION FOR ECONOMIC CO-OPERATION AND DEVELOPMENT

Pursuant to Article 1 of the Convention signed in Paris on 14th December 1960, and which came into force on 30th September 1961, the Organisation for Economic Co-operation and Development (OECD) shall promote policies designed:

- to achieve the highest sustainable economic growth and employment and a rising standard of living in Member countries, while maintaining financial stability, and thus to contribute to the development of the world economy;
- to contribute to sound economic expansion in Member as well as non-member countries in the process of economic development; and
- to contribute to the expansion of world trade on a multilateral, non-discriminatory basis in accordance with international obligations.

The original Member countries of the OECD are Austria, Belgium, Canada, Denmark, France, Germany, Greece, Iceland, Ireland, Italy, Luxembourg, the Netherlands, Norway, Portugal, Spain, Sweden, Switzerland, Turkey, the United Kingdom and the United States. The following countries became Members subsequently through accession at the dates indicated hereafter: Japan (28th April 1964), Finland (28th January 1969), Australia (7th June 1971), New Zealand (29th May 1973) and Mexico (18th May 1994). The Commission of the European Communities takes part in the work of the OECD (Article 13 of the OECD Convention).

Publié également en français.

Table of contents

Tables

Diagrams

Annexes

BASIC STATISTICS OF CANADA

THE LAND

Area (thousand sq. km)	9 976	Population of major cities, including	
Agricultural area (1990, as per cent		metropolitan areas, 1991 (thousands)	
of total area)	6.4	Montréal	3 127
		Toronto	3 893

THE PEOPLE

Population (1993)	28 890 100	Civilian labour force (1993)	13 945 800
Number of inhabitants per sq. km	2.9	Employment agriculture (1993)	448 900
Population, annual net natural		Immigration (annual average 1989-1993)	228 916
increase (average 1989-1993)	201 100	Average annual increase in civilian	
Natural increase rate per 1 000		labour force (1989-1993, per cent)	1.0
inhabitants (average 1989-1993)	7.3		

PRODUCTION

GDP in 1993 (millions of Canadian dollars)	718 658	Origin of gross domestic product	
GDP per head (Canadian dollars)	24 633	(1993, per cent of total, 1986 prices):	
Gross fixed investment (private and public)		Agricultural, forestry and fishing	2.8
per head (Canadian dollars)	4 394	Mining and quarrying	4.2
Gross fixed investment (private and public)		Manufacturing	17.9
as per cent of GDP	17.8	Construction	5.1
		Non business sector	18.1
		Other	54.6

THE GOVERNMENT

			House	
Government current expenditure on goods		Composition of Parliament	House	
and services (1993, as per cent of GDP)	21.5	(October 1993):	of	Senate
Government gross fixed capital formation		(number of seats)	Commons	
(1993, as per cent of GDP)	2.3			
Federal Government current revenue		Progressive Conservative	153	53
(1993, as per cent of GDP)	19.3	Liberal	79	48
Federal direct and guaranteed debt (1993,		New Democratic	43	-
per cent of current expenditure)	231.1	Bloc québécois	8	-
		Independent	3	5
		Reform	1	1

FOREIGN TRADE

Exports (1993)		Imports (1993)	
Exports of goods and services,		Imports of goods and services,	
as per cent of GDP	29.3	as per cent of GDP	29.9
Main exports (per cent of commodity exports):		Main imports (per cent of commodity imports):	
Wheat	1.6	Industrial materials	17.1
Natural gas	3	Motor vehicles and parts	23.3
Lumber and sawmill products	6.2	Producers' equipment	30.9
Pulp and paper	6.8	Consumer goods	12.4
Other metals and minerals	9.8	Main suppliers (per cent	
Motor vehicles and parts	26.5	of commodity imports):	
Other manufactured goods	25.3	United States	73.2
Main customers (per cent of commodity exports):		EEC	8.1
United States	80.2	Japan	4.9
EEC	6.1		
Japan	4.5		

THE CURRENCY

Monetary unit: Canadian dollar	Currency unit per US dollar,	
	average of daily figures:	
	year 1993	1.290

Note: An international comparison of certain basic statistics is given in an annex table.

Introduction

The economic recovery in Canada has gained momentum and broadened since 1993, with household spending now adding to continued strong business investment and external demand (notably from the United States). Employment is rising and had virtually regained its pre-recession level by mid-1994, although the unemployment rate – albeit receding – is still in double digits. Aided by substantial slack in the economy, inflation has continued to be subdued, despite the downward adjustment of the Canadian dollar since 1992. Notwithstanding the buoyancy of exports, the current-account deficit has remained large, reflecting an ongoing high import propensity and the cost of servicing Canada's large external debt.

Economic growth is projected to strengthen further over the next eighteen months, but not sufficiently to fully close the large output gap that emerged during the recession. As a result, and given a continuing excess supply of labour, inflation is expected to remain low. In addition, with improved competitiveness underpinning export growth and some rise in the terms of trade, the current-account deficit should narrow gradually. However, the strength of the recovery could be adversely affected by financial-market disturbances. In recent months, the tightening of US monetary policy, along with concerns about fiscal and political developments in Canada, have led to exchange-rate weakness and upward pressure on interest rates. Given Canada's favourable inflation perform-ance, such pressures should eventually unwind, although savers and investors are likely to continue to demand substantial risk premiums as long as federal and provincial finances are not perceived to be sound.

Following some progress in fiscal consolidation in the second half of the 1980s, the general government deficit has widened again, reaching 7 per cent of GDP in 1993. As a result, the public debt-to-GDP ratio has grown sharply, and now exceeds the OECD average by a wide margin. The increased attention given by financial markets to these developments is reflected in high long-term interest rates, relative both to inflation and to their counterparts in the United States. The federal government has set a deficit target of 3 per cent of GDP by 1996/97 as a first step towards fiscal balance, and most provinces intend to balance their – overall or current account – budgets over the medium term. However, with higher-than-expected interest rates putting upward pressure on debt servicing costs, the attainment of these deficit targets is likely to require additional consolidation efforts. While fiscal restraint may moderate domestic demand in the short run, it would ease the operation of monetary policy, by allowing reductions in interest rates consistent with Canada's low inflation, thereby improving conditions for a sustained growth of activity.

Part I of the Survey examines the main factors underlying recent economic developments and discusses the short-term outlook. Part II reviews both macroeconomic and structural policies, with particular attention given to the fiscal situation. Part III contains a special study of the Canadian income-security system – which is currently being reviewed by the federal government – indicating possible avenues for reform. Conclusions arising from the analysis in the Survey are presented in Part IV.

I.   Recent trends and short-term prospects

A progressive upturn

The recovery of economic activity that began in the spring of 1991 has strengthened over the past year (Diagram 1). Fuelled initially by foreign demand and business spending on machinery and equipment, it is now showing signs of broadening to the household sector, as rising employment boosts consumer confidence and private consumption. The substantial slack in product and labour markets that had emerged in the early 1990s has virtually eliminated wage and price pressures. Along with robust corporate investment, this paves the way for sustained non-inflationary growth. At the same time, the significant improvement in Canada's competitive position in recent years should allow a gradual unwinding of the large external deficit.

Despite its recent acceleration, the upturn has remained slow by historical standards and has significantly lagged behind that in the United States. As a result, the two economies are now out of synchronisation to an unusual extent. While little spare capacity is left in the US economy, the output gap in Canada is generally estimated at around 5 per cent. It has taken over three years of recovery for employment to regain its pre-recession level (Diagram 1) and unemployment has come down only gradually from the peak reached in 1992, in spite of continued depressed labour-force participation.

As discussed in last year's Survey, the gradual nature of the recovery can in part be traced to the fact that the current cycle has lacked a strong catalyst – such as an inventory-driven rebound in production or a surge in *net* exports – to jump start the economy. Indeed, the growth stimulus from rising exports to the United States has been dampened by strong imports. The sharp increase in two-way trade reflects, among other things, the influence of globalisation and market liberalisation, including the implementation of the Free Trade Agreement with

11

Diagram 1. **KEY ASPECTS OF ECONOMIC ACTIVITY**

GDP and total domestic demand
Volume, 1982 = 100 (semi-log scale)

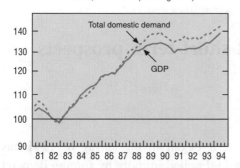

GDP deflator and unit labour costs[1]
% change over previous quarter, annual rates

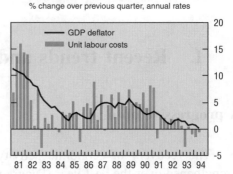

Total labour force and employment
1982 = 100 (semi-log scale)

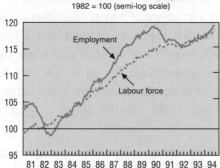

Terms of trade and effective exchange rate
1986 = 100

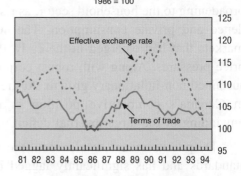

**General government net lending
and external balance** (% of GDP)

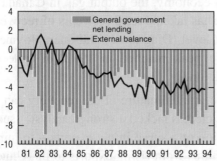

Real short term interest rate[2]
Per cent

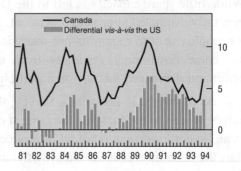

1. Total economy.
2. 90-day commercial paper rate, deflated by the GDP deflator.
Source: CANSIM – Statistics Canada.

12

the United States. The high import propensity also reflects the high value of the Canadian dollar in the early 1990s and the composition of domestic demand (see below). The easing of monetary conditions after 1991 was gradual but gathered momentum as it became clear that inflation was falling to the lower end of the target ranges. It was, however, interrupted or temporarily reversed by several episodes of financial-market concerns about rising government deficits and debt and constitutional uncertainties. While this may have slowed the recovery, the marked easing of monetary conditions through 1993 and into early 1994 has clearly played a role in the pick-up in growth in 1994.

Another factor that has probably exerted some drag on the recovery is industrial restructuring. Recent research (see below) does not support the view that there has been an abnormal amount of "output restructuring", *i.e.* change in industry output and employment shares. Instead, there is evidence of "input restructuring", *i.e.* substitution of capital for labour, resulting from declines in the user cost of capital combined with a sluggish adjustment of real wages to the slack in labour markets. This has been reflected in the foreign balance, given the high import content of machinery and equipment investment, as well as in meagre job creation relative to output. Slow employment growth, in turn, raised job insecurity to unprecedented levels and acted to depress consumer confidence, a trend that has begun reversing only more recently.

While most of the factors that have slowed the recovery are ebbing, some of them may persist for some time. Thus, input restructuring, *i.e.* capital/labour substitution, is already showing signs of abating. Recent strong employment growth is likely to have significantly alleviated fears on the part of those already employed about possible job loss. At the same time, strong investment in machinery and equipment has laid the foundations for sustained non-inflationary growth. Moreover, the effective exchange rate has depreciated sharply (Diagram 1) and – contrary to the situation prevailing in the early 1990s – the Canadian dollar is now well below estimates of purchasing power parity. Restored international competitiveness should lead to a substitution of domestic production for imports and to a gain in export-market share. On the other hand, financial-market disturbances may continue to have an adverse effect on the recovery. Indeed, despite encouraging signs most recently, the tightening in monetary conditions in the spring of 1994 could take longer to fully unwind than previous comparable episodes, such as that of the autumn of 1992 when concerns about fiscal and political developments also led to a marked firming of interest rates. However, both short-term interest rates and the exchange rate are now considerably lower than at times of earlier financial-market disturbances, and the economic recovery has become more robust since.

The rest of this chapter examines in more detail recent economic developments resulting from these various influences and discusses the short-term economic outlook. The policy setting impacting on recent and future economic performance is reviewed in the next chapter of the Survey.

Characteristics of the current recovery

Continued buoyancy of exports

The pursuit of recovery has been based on continued strong growth of exports (Table 1). From 1991 to 1993, the share of exports in GDP increased by 5 percentage points to 29½ per cent. While capacity utilisation in total non-farm goods producing industries is still well below its long-term average, the majority of export-oriented industries are operating at above average rates (albeit still significantly below previous peak rates). The major source of export growth has been strong demand from the United States: exports to the United States rose from just under 76 per cent of total Canadian merchandise exports in 1991 to over 81 per cent in 1993. With disinflation and currency depreciation restoring competitiveness, Canada's exporters gained market share in 1993 following several years of deteriorating export performance. However, as noted above, imports have been buoyant too (Table 1). Partly reflecting the composition of aggregate demand, the overall import propensity has remained high even though Canadian suppliers' competitive position in domestic markets has also improved significantly. As a result, the growth contribution of the change in the real foreign balance has been relatively limited (Diagram 2), averaging ½ percentage point per annum during the recovery.

Gradual strengthening of domestic demand

While export volumes have grown by more than one-third since the recession bottomed out in 1991, real domestic demand has just increased by some 5 per cent, exceeding its pre-recession level only from late 1993 (Diagram 1).

Table 1. **Demand and output**

Volume percentage change, annual rates

	$\frac{1979}{1973}$	$\frac{1989}{1979}$	1990	1991	1992	1993	$\frac{Q1\ 1994}{Q4\ 1993}$	$\frac{Q2\ 1994}{Q1\ 1994}$
Private consumption	4.4	3.1	1.0	−1.5	1.3	1.6	4.4	3.0
Government consumption	3.5	2.5	3.2	2.8	1.2	0.5	−3.3	−2.4
Gross fixed investment	5.1	5.3	−3.5	−2.2	−2.8	−0.2	1.5	18.2
Public	−0.3	3.8	6.9	4.7	−0.6	4.4	−0.1	13.5
Private	5.9	5.5	−4.8	−3.1	−3.2	−0.9	1.8	18.9
Residential	3.4	4.5	−9.7	−12.5	7.9	−4.4	3.0	18.4
Non residential	6.8	5.3	−2.4	1.1	−7.5	0.7	1.3	19.1
Final domestic demand	**4.3**	**3.5**	**0.4**	**−0.8**	**0.4**	**1.0**	**2.2**	**4.9**
Stockbuilding [1]	0.1	−0.1	−1.0	−0.2	−0.1	0.8	−0.4	0.6
Total domestic demand	**4.4**	**3.4**	**−0.5**	**−1.0**	**0.3**	**1.8**	**1.8**	**5.6**
Exports of goods and services	4.6	5.2	4.1	1.0	7.7	10.4	4.6	18.2
Imports of goods and services	6.0	6.4	2.0	3.1	5.9	8.8	0.8	15.1
Foreign balance [1]	−0.2	−0.4	0.6	−0.7	0.4	0.3	1.3	0.7
Error of estimate [1]	0.1	0.0	−0.2	−0.2	−0.1	0.0	1.2	0
GDP at market prices	**4.2**	**3.1**	**−0.2**	**−1.8**	**0.6**	**2.2**	**4.4**	**6.4**
of which:								
Agriculture	−0.2	2.3	3.1	−3.5	−5.0	6.8	0.5	4.3
Mining	−4.1	1.0	−0.3	1.9	1.8	6.9	−1.8	24.1
Manufacturing	2.5	2.1	−3.7	−6.9	0.7	5.0	1.4	11.7
Construction	4.5	3.4	−0.3	−7.8	−8.5	−4.8	−3.9	15.7
Services	4.8	3.4	0.6	0	1.6	2.2	4.5	2.5

1. Contribution to GDP volume growth.
Source: Statistics Canada; OECD, *Quarterly National Accounts.*

The gradual upturn of domestic demand reflects widely diverging developments in its major components: while growth in government consumption has slowed, turning negative most recently (Table 1), private consumer spending showed a relatively steady upward trend before gaining momentum of late; residential investment rebounded early in the recovery but has weakened thereafter; the decline in business construction has begun to be reversed only recently; on the other hand, as noted, business investment in machinery and equipment has shown surprising strength, exceeding its pre-recession level from late 1992, one year earlier than private consumption.

Diagram 2. **CONTRIBUTIONS TO CHANGES IN GDP**

Per cent changes over 4 quarters

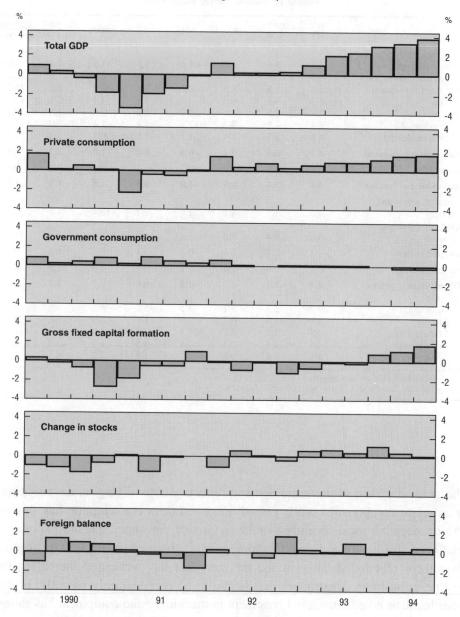

Source: OECD.

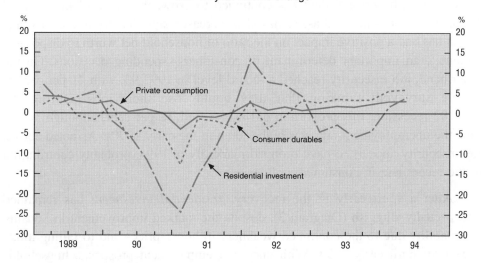

Diagram 3. **HOUSEHOLD DEMAND**
Year-on-year volume change

Source: CANSIM – Statistics Canada.

While contributing steadily to the recovery (Diagram 2), *private consumption* has proved much less supportive than in the past. The modest pace of consumer spending reflects the fact that up to mid-1993 it largely followed low disposable income growth, with the household saving ratio remaining broadly stable. This has changed, however, over the last year or so. Initially, households appear to have lowered their saving ratio to offset the adverse effect on disposable income of the substantial personal-income tax increases in some provinces in mid-1993. While rebounding in early 1994, the household saving ratio has nonetheless remained at a lower level, despite a pick-up in disposable incomes. As a result, consumer spending – in particular on durables (Diagram 3) – has strengthened, although there are some signs of slowing growth in household demand related to recent interest increases and ongoing job uncertainty in sectors still vulnerable to restructuring.

The unusual stability of the household saving ratio during the first two years of the current recovery appears to be attributable to widespread job insecurity, which tended to offset the downward pressure on savings from factors such as

17

rising net wealth, lower inflation, and – to a lesser extent – lower real interest rates. Although personal debt has continued to grow, the value of households' financial and non-financial assets has also increased significantly in recent years, which has had a positive impact on the ratio of household net worth to disposable income – an important determinant of consumers' spending decisions. On the other hand, job insecurity reached a record level in 1992-93, with 41 per cent of people surveyed[1] thinking that they could lose their jobs. During the 1981-82 recession, this proportion did not exceed 32 per cent, although at that time the unemployment rate was higher than in the early 1990s. As noted above, job insecurity appears to have dropped markedly in 1994, probably contributing to the recent rise in consumer confidence.

After a spurt early in the recovery, *residential investment* has remained unexpectedly sluggish (Diagram 3), despite the marked improvement in housing affordability due to the continued weakness in house prices and to falling mortgage rates until early 1994. With uncertain employment prospects, households appear to have been reluctant to make major spending commitments. Moreover, revised population statistics suggest a much more cyclical pattern to the underlying demographic demand for housing than thought before.[2] Consequently, the number of housing starts needed to meet demographic requirements, which had been put at about 200 000, is now estimated to be in the 180 000 range. With actual housing starts having more or less mirrored swings in estimated underlying demographic demand, pent-up demand for housing appears to be limited. Still, a rebound in immigration in recent quarters points to an increase in residential investment to meet demographic requirements, despite rising mortgage rates. The initial effect of the recent hike in mortgage rates was to moderate the decline in house resales since April 1994, as buyers with pre-approved mortgages at lower interest rates rushed into the market.

The behaviour of *business fixed investment* in recent years has been influenced by two divergent developments (Diagram 4). Given sizeable surplus capacity and depressed prices in commercial real estate, spending on structures declined markedly for about three years before rebounding most recently. On the other hand, despite low corporate cash flow, investment in machinery and equipment has been unusually strong, both compared with previous periods of economic weakness and developments in other countries. This is all the more remarkable as it follows upon a 70 per cent rise between 1983 and 1989. A tax

Diagram 4. **BUSINESS FIXED INVESTMENT**
Constant prices

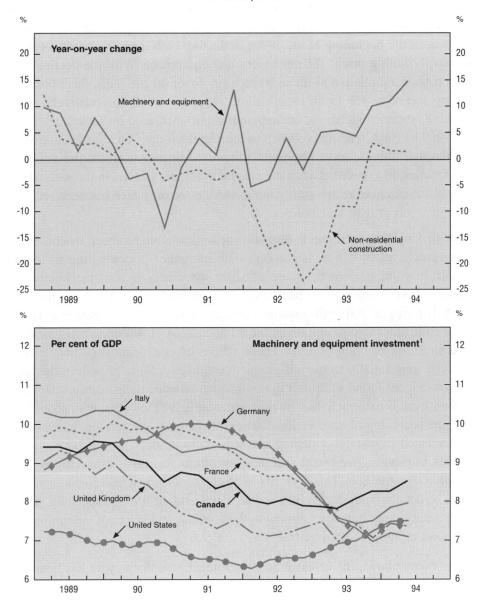

1. Including public sector.
Source: CANSIM – Statistics Canada; OECD, *Quarterly National Accounts.*

19

credit for small businesses that incurred machinery and equipment investments from December 1992 through December 1993 appears to have played a role. More important, however, has been a one-third reduction in the user cost of capital since the beginning of the 1990s, reflecting both lower real costs of funds and sharply falling prices for machinery and equipment. With the decline even more pronounced relative to the average wage (over 40 per cent), there has been a strong incentive for firms to substitute cheaper capital for relatively more-expensive labour.[3] Indeed, the capital/labour ratio increased by some 20 per cent from 1989 to 1993, lending credence to the view that the Canadian economy has gone through one the most important periods of (input) restructuring since the War. A major difference between the present cycle and the one in the early 1980s has been the extent of restructuring in the service sector, which has been reflected in sluggish job growth (see below).

A striking feature of recent business capital spending has been its concentration in purchases of office machinery: with computer prices falling by nearly one-half, in volume terms the share of office machinery in total machinery and equipment investment has doubled since the late 1980s, to more than one-third. As noted above, the fall in the cost of machinery and equipment relative to labour has led companies to concentrate on reducing costs by substituting equipment for labour in the production process. These efficiency-enhancing investments have not added substantially to overall productive capacity. Slow growth in the latter has been evident in the sharp fall in non-residential construction, to levels where net investment is extremely low by post-war standards. However, with profits and sales prospects improving, rationalisation investment should be increasingly complemented by capital-widening investment, as evident in the sharp upward revisions to private investment spending intentions for 1994, especially in non-residential construction. This is in line with the observation that business spending on structures started reviving towards the end of 1993, especially in the energy sector and industry, although there is no evidence of an immediate turnaround in commercial construction.

As noted above, the absence of a significant inventory cycle has been one reason for the modest pace of the current recovery. Although *stockbuilding* has started contributing to economic growth over the past eighteen months or so (Diagram 2), the stock/output ratio has continued to decline. As can be seen from Diagram 5, a major break in the trend of the inventory-to-sales ratio occurred

Diagram 5. **BUSINESS NON-FARM INVENTORY-TO-SALES RATIO**

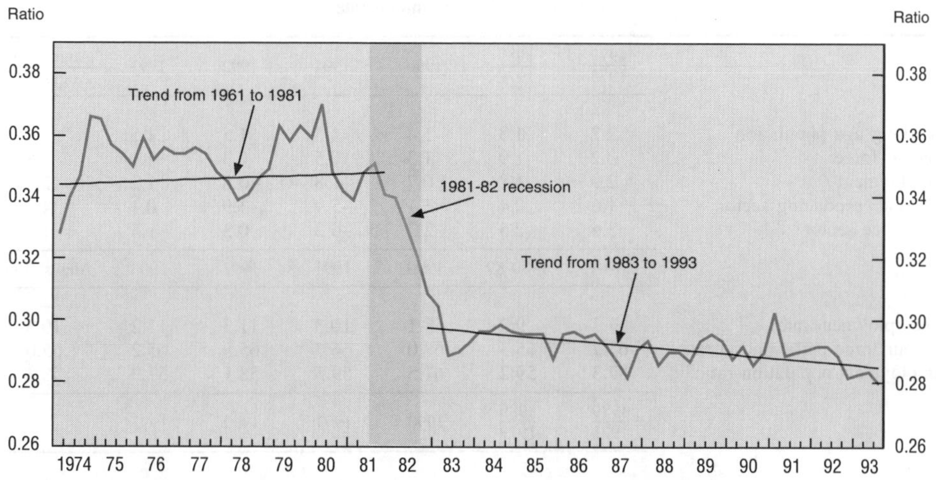

Ratio

0.38

Trend from 1961 to 1981

0.36

0.34

1981-82 recession

0.32

Trend from 1983 to 1993

0.30

0.28

0.26

1974 75   76   77   78   79   80   81   82   83   84   85   86   87   88   89   90   91   92   93

Source: Ministry of Finance.

during the 1981-82 recession, when businesses massively cut their stocks in response to high real interest rates. Since then, the stock/output ratio has displayed a downward trend and tended to fluctuate much less than before. The major factor behind both the downtrend and relative stability of the ratio seems to have been the increasing adoption of computer technology, which has allowed for considerable efficiency gains in stock management.

Persistent labour market slack

Labour-market slack has remained substantial, with unemployment still well above its ''natural rate''. Although the latter appears to have increased somewhat since the late 1980s, when it had fallen to around 8 per cent, this largely reflects effects of the severe recession which will tend to reverse themselves.[4] After rising sharply during the 1990-91 recession, the unemployment rate continued to drift upwards during the early phase of the recovery, peaking at 11½ per cent in late 1992. Remaining above 11 per cent through 1993, it dropped below that level only in the spring of 1994. Despite a marked decline more recently, the unemployment rate is still in double digits (Table 2). This reflects an increased

21

Table 2. **Labour supply and demand**

Percentage change, annual rates

	$\frac{1979}{1973}$	$\frac{1989}{1979}$	1990	1991	1992	1993	$\frac{\text{August 1994}}{\text{August 1993}}$
Working age population	2.2	1.3	1.4	1.5	1.5	1.5	1.4
Labour force	3.2	1.9	1.3	0.5	0.3	1.1	1.3
Employment	2.9	1.8	0.7	−1.8	−0.8	1.2	2.4
Goods producing sector	1.6	0.4	−3.1	−5.9	−3.9	0.1	4.1
Service sector	3.6	2.5	2.2	−0.3	0.3	1.5	1.8
	1974-79	1980-89	1990	1991	1992	1993	August 1994
Unemployment rate [1]	7.2	9.3	8.1	10.3	11.3	11.2	10.3
Labour force participation rate [2]	61.7	65.3	67.0	66.3	65.5	65.2	65.0
Employment/population ratio [2]	57.3	59.2	61.5	59.5	58.1	57.9	58.3
	$\frac{1979}{1973}$	$\frac{1989}{1979}$	1990	1991	1992	1993	
Memorandum items:							
Labour productivity	1.3	1.3	−0.9	0.0	1.4	1.0	
Total factor productivity [3]	0.8	0.3	0.1 [4]	0.0 [4]	0.0 [4]	0.1 [4]	

1. Per cent of labour force.
2. Per cent of population 15 years and over.
3. Business sector.
4. Trend growth.
Source: Statistics Canada; OECD.

duration of unemployment: its incidence (*i.e.* the proportion of workers experiencing any unemployment spell over a twelve-month period) has already declined to near the pre-recession level. Despite unusually slow employment growth during the current recovery, the unemployment rate is currently not higher than at the same stage of the much stronger recovery of the early 1980s. This is due to a marked and prolonged decline in the labour-force participation rate.

Such a phenomenon is unprecedented in the post-war period. During the 1981-82 recession the drop in the participation rate was relatively limited and reversed after one year as "discouraged" workers re-entered an improving job market. Since the beginning of 1990, the participation rate has fallen by around 2½ percentage points – a trend which has continued well into the recovery (Table 2). Contrary to the early 1980s, the decline in labour-force participation during the 1990-91 recession was not associated with a sharp rise in the number of "discouraged" workers as officially measured by Statistical Canada. Previous empirical analysis suggests that cyclical factors, notably the decline in employment opportunities, account for around 1 percentage point of the recent reduction in the participation rate, the remainder being explained by a number of structural factors. First, rates of income taxation have risen well above their trend, reducing after-tax income and labour supply. Second, payroll taxes paid by employees – in particular unemployment-insurance premiums – have reduced the supply of labour. Third, since 1990 training programmes for the unemployed have been stepped up substantially, and people on such programmes are less likely to be in the labour force than those not being trained. Fourth, several changes to unemployment-insurance regulations which reduced eligibility and the generosity of the system (see Part II) may have caused people to withdraw from the labour force. Finally, there has been a significant increase in the number of full-time students, which appears too large to be fully explained by the cyclical decline in job opportunities and might reflect increased recognition of the payoff of more extensive education. While the curb on unemployment-insurance premiums announced in the 1994 Budget should reduce downward pressure on labour-force participation, some of these factors may persist for some time, lowering the unemployment rate – but also potential output.

Whereas low labour-force participation has damped unemployment, unusually weak employment growth – the so-called "jobless recovery" – has tended to keep it high. Unlike in the previous cycle, when employment dropped and recovered sharply, employment was still below its pre-recession level three years into the present recovery (Diagram 6), although it has since caught up. The major factor behind this employment weakness is the slower pace of output growth. Indeed, the rise of real GDP during the current upswing has been only one-third of that achieved over the corresponding period of the preceding recovery in the 1980s. But what is normally meant by a "jobless recovery" is that employment is weaker than warranted by its traditional relationship with output. At first glance, productivity gains do not appear to have been outstanding in recent years, except in manufacturing (Diagram 6). However, since productivity gains early in recoveries reflect output increases leading to better use of under-utilised workers, account should be taken of output growth when assessing productivity performance. Relative to this benchmark, productivity gains have been unusually strong:

Diagram 6. **A JOBLESS RECOVERY**

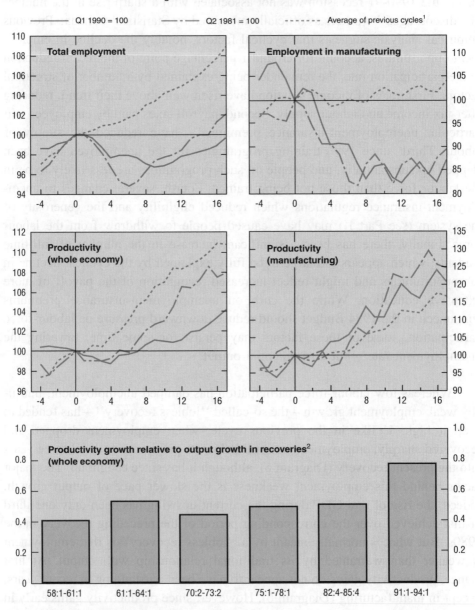

Q1 1990 = 100 ——— Q2 1981 = 100 - - - - - - Average of previous cycles[1]

Total employment

Employment in manufacturing

**Productivity
(whole economy)**

**Productivity
(manufacturing)**

**Productivity growth relative to output growth in recoveries[2]
(whole economy)**

58:1-61:1　61:1-64:1　70:2-73:2　75:1-78:1　82:4-85:4　91:1-94:1

1. Cyclical peaks (Q1 1951, Q2 1953, Q4 1956, Q1 1961, Q1 1964, Q1 1974) = 100.
2. First three years from cyclical trough.
Source: OECD, *National Accounts, Main Economic Indicators.*

while in past recoveries about half of the increase in output came from productivity growth and the other half from higher employment, during the current upturn about 80 per cent of output growth has been the result of more efficient use of labour and only around 20 per cent of increased employment (Diagram 6). As discussed above, one reason for the "jobless recovery" has been a technology-driven shock to the price of physical capital, encouraging employers to substitute capital for labour. Another factor dampening labour demand has been the emergence of an unprecedented gap between actual real producer wages and those warranted on the basis of labour productivity due in part to strong increases in employer-paid payroll taxes (see below).

Low inflation

With a continued substantial output gap, inflation has remained subdued despite a significant depreciation of the Canadian dollar. The annual change in the consumer price index (CPI) – virtually zero in recent months (Diagram 7) – understates inflation trends, however, as it reflects a sharp cut in tobacco taxes designed to curb cigarette smuggling across Canada's border with the United States. Abstracting from this, underlying CPI inflation is of the order of $1\frac{1}{2}$ per cent. This is still at the lower end of the official target range (see Part II) and surprisingly modest given the 18 per cent decline in the effective exchange rate since 1991. Simple rules of thumb based on import propensities suggest that such an exchange-rate depreciation could, over time, be expected to raise the consumer-price level by more than 5 per cent. An offsetting factor has been a decline in unit labour costs – as a result of the output gap – over the past year or so. In addition, because of sluggish demand (until recently) and strong competitive pressures in retail trade, increases in input prices have apparently not been passed on to consumers and, instead, have been absorbed in profit margins. The exchange-rate effect on prices of imported goods is, however, already visible on the producer-price level (Diagram 7), where better demand conditions seem to have allowed an improvement in profit margins in some sectors. Improving world demand has led to a strengthening of commodity prices and, hence, Canadian industrial product prices.

Wage inflation has subsided steadily since 1991, reaching historically low levels in early 1994 (Table 3). Since then, it has picked up somewhat, with the annual increase in effective earnings exceeding 2 per cent, although wage settle-

Diagram 7. **INFLATION INDICATORS**
Percentage change over 12 months

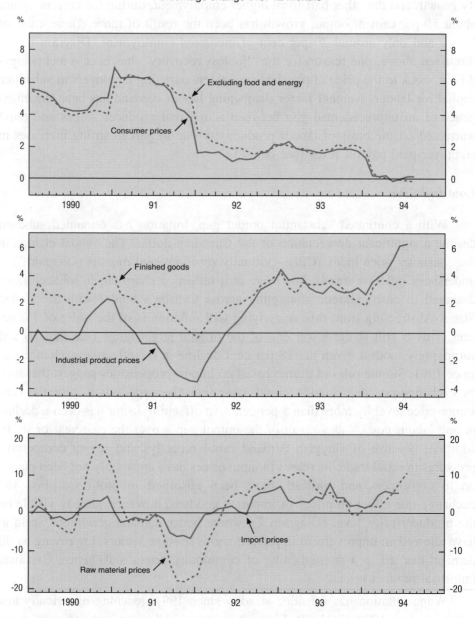

Source: CANSIM – Statistics Canada.

ments have remained subdued. While nominal wage growth has declined markedly, inflation has fallen even faster, implying a continued rise in *real* wages despite sizeable labour-market slack. Beginning in the late 1980s, growth in real producer wages – that is, nominal wage costs deflated by producer prices – has outstripped that of labour productivity by a wide margin. By 1993, a "real producer wage gap" of 7 per cent had emerged, with increases in non-wage labour costs (in particular payroll taxes) contributing 4 percentage points. The stickiness of real wages along with tax increases has been reflected in a sharp fall in the profit share in the early 1990s as well as weak growth in employment

Table 3. **Wages, prices and profits**

Percentage change, annual rates

	$\dfrac{1979}{1973}$	$\dfrac{1989}{1979}$	1990	1991	1992	1993	$\dfrac{\text{Q1 1994}}{\text{Q1 1993}}$	$\dfrac{\text{Q2 1994}}{\text{Q2 1993}}$
Wages								
Compensation per employee	10.8	6.7	4.8	4.8	3.5	2.1	1.0	1.4
Wage rate (business sector)	10.1	6.9	3.1	2.9	2.3	1.6	1.2	..
Hourly earnings in manufacturing	11.6	6.1	4.7	4.7	3.5	2.1	1.5	1.9
Major collective settlements	..	6.7	5.8	3.8	2.4	0.8	0.6	0.1
Unit labour costs	**9.3**	**5.6**	**5.5**	**4.5**	**1.8**	**0.3**	**–1.4**	**–0.7**
Manufacturing	9.4	4.9	3.4	4.1	–1.2	–2.3	0	..
Profits								
Pre-tax	14.8	5.3	–25.4	–24.8	–1.9	20.3	37.5	30.2
After-tax	15.2	4.0	–42.9	–39.2	1.7	54.2	51.5	36.6
Per unit of output	10.6	1.9	–24.7	–22.9	–2.7	16.6	32.2	24.6
Prices								
GDP deflator (current weights)	9.2	5.7	3.1	2.7	1.4	1.1	0.8	0.2
GDP deflator (fixed weights)	9.8	6.0	3.4	3.2	1.3	1.6	0.8	0.5
Consumer price index	9.2	6.5	4.8	5.6	1.5	1.8	0.6	0
Private consumption deflator	8.6	6.1	4.3	4.8	1.3	1.7	1.2	0.7
Import price deflator	10.7	2.0	1.1	–2.3	2.2	4.6	3.7	6.0
New housing price index	..	..	1.5	–6.9	0.0	1.2	0.8	0

Source: Statistics Canada; OECD, *National Accounts.*

relative to output. Although further wage moderation, along with a pick-up in producer prices over the past year, has led to an improvement in profitability, the substantial real wage overhang may well continue to limit labour demand for some time.

Large external deficit

The conditions underlying Canada's external position have improved in recent years. By the early 1990s, the country was faced with a serious competitiveness problem resulting from relatively high wage growth, weak productivity performance and exchange-rate appreciation since the mid-1980s. The reversal of these trends is reflected in a significant decline in relative export prices in common currency terms, restoring the competitive position prevailing in the mid-1980s (Diagram 8). With relative unit labour costs falling markedly more recently, the export sector's profitability – as measured by the relative profit margin indicator – has also started improving, although it still falls short of the levels recorded in the 1980s. Moreover, as the recovery in Canada has significantly lagged behind that in the United States, the country's relative demand position (Diagram 8) has been favourable to the foreign balance. Nevertheless, so far, the current-account deficit has remained large, fluctuating around 4 per cent of GDP since the late 1980s, as improvements in the trade balance have just been sufficient to offset the rise in the invisibles deficit, reflecting the cost of servicing Canada's substantial external debt.

Canada's traditional merchandise trade surplus has tended to widen since 1991, driven by a marked rise in the large bilateral surplus with the United States. The improvement in the trade account has been slower, however, than in previous cycles, leaving the surplus well below the levels achieved in the first half of the 1980s (Diagram 8). As noted above, this reflects buoyant import growth despite weak domestic demand. Indeed, in 1993 the volume increase in imports (around 10 per cent) matched that of exports. At the same time, with import prices rising almost as much as export prices ($4\frac{1}{2}$ and $5\frac{1}{2}$ per cent, respectively), the terms of trade provided only little support to the trade balance. Rapid export growth is largely attributable to the strength of activity in the United States, although improved international competitiveness appears to have arrested the loss in real export market share observed since the late 1980s. According to OECD Secretariat estimates, for manufactures significant market gains were already

Diagram 8. **THE CURRENT BALANCE AND ITS MAJOR COMPONENTS**

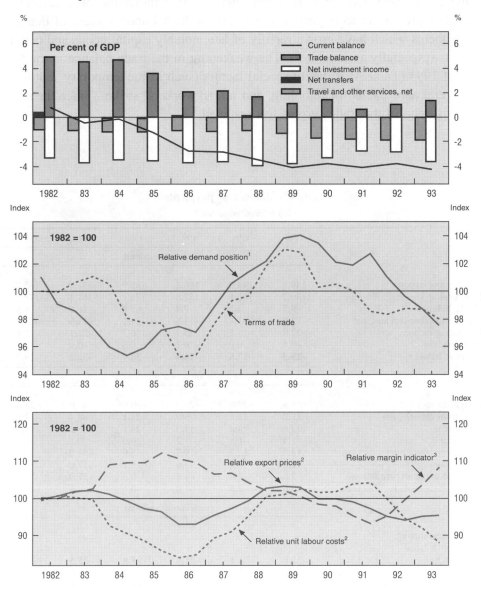

1. Index of Canadian final domestic demand divided by an export share weighted index of final domestic demand of major trading partners.
2. In manufacturing. Common currency.
3. Ratio of relative export prices to relative unit labour costs.
Source: CANSIM – Statistics Canada; OECD, *National Accounts,* Secretariat estimates.

achieved in 1993. On the other hand, there is little indication of a decline in Canada's propensity to import. This reflects the high import content of demand components which have grown rapidly of late, notably capital goods and certain exports (especially automobiles). The weakening in the trade balance in the first half of 1994 (Table 4) is due to special factors (such as the temporary shutdown of several auto plants for retooling, and a dockworkers' strike). Since then, the upward trend in the trade surplus has resumed.

Table 4.　**Balance of payments**[1]

C$ billion, annualised

	1990	1991	1992	1993	1994 Q1	1994 Q2
	Seasonally-adjusted					
Merchandise exports	149.8	144.3	160.1	185.9	178.0	182.7
Merchandise imports	140.2	140.1	152.8	176.1	167.1	173.2
Trade balance	**9.7**	**4.2**	**7.4**	**9.8**	**10.8**	**9.5**
Travel and other services, net	−12.0	−12.7	−13.6	−14.1	−14.9	−13.7
Investment income, net	−22.8	−19.1	−20.1	−26.7	−27.1	−25.4
Transfers, net	−0.1	0.0	0.1	0.3	−0.9	0.5
Current balance	**−25.3**	**−27.6**	**−26.4**	**−30.7**	**−32.2**	**−29.2**
	Not seasonally-adjusted					
Current balance	−25.3	−27.6	−26.3	−30.6	−40.0	−28.6
Long-term capital[2], net	12.2	12.5	9.6	24.1	88.4	12.8
Private	13.6	14.2	11.3	24.1	88.2	13.3
Official[3]	−1.4	−1.8	−1.7	0.0	0.1	−0.5
Short-term capital, net	13.7	12.3	9.7	5.9	−44.0	8.3
Non-monetary[4]	11.0	7.9	14.6	6.2	−17.0	6.2
Private monetary institutions	2.6	4.4	−4.8	−0.3	−27.0	2.1
Change in reserves (+ = increase)	0.6	−2.8	−7.0	−0.6	4.4	−7.5
	Seasonally-adjusted					
Memorandum items:						
Current balance						
US$ billion	−21.6	−24.1	−21.9	−23.8	−25.5	−23.0
Per cent of GDP	−3.8	−4.1	−3.8	−4.3	−4.6	−4.1

1.　OECD/IMF definitions.
2.　Excludes special transactions.
3.　Including portfolio transactions of public authorities and Canadian Government utilisation of revolving standby credit facilities with domestic and foreign banks.
4.　Including errors and omissions.
Source: OECD.

Nonetheless, Canada's overall external disequilibrium has persisted, due to a sizeable deficit on non-merchandise transactions, and in particular on investment income associated with the country's high and growing net foreign liability position. Although falling interest rates have damped the rise in debt servicing costs, the investment income deficit has resumed its upward trend over the past two years or so (Table 4). This reflects a pick-up in profits on foreign direct investment in Canada, following a decline in dividend payments of Canadian firms to foreigners during the recession of 1990-92. One area where the lower Canadian dollar is already having some positive effects is cross-border shopping and the travel account more generally: the upward trend in the deficit on travel and other services observed since the late 1980s appears to have been reversed in recent quarters (Table 4).

Short-term outlook

Economic growth is projected to average 4 per cent in 1994 and 1995 (Table 5). Strong export growth seems set to continue both because Canada's export markets are expected to expand rapidly and because the marked improvement in international competitiveness – about 20 per cent since 1991 in terms of relative unit labour costs – should allow Canadian exporters to gain market share. Business investment should remain buoyant, fuelled by rising profits and strong export demand, and household expenditure is also expected to gather momentum, as employment growth boosts disposable incomes and rising consumer confidence leads to some decline in the saving ratio. More generally, the significant fall in interest rates over the last few years should support domestic spending. Despite the projected pick-up in employment, the decline in unemployment is likely to be gradual, as labour-force participation is expected to recover following its pronounced cyclical fall. With persistent labour-market slack, wage increases are projected to remain moderate, implying little growth in unit labour costs. Nevertheless, inflation is likely to rise somewhat, reflecting the effects of earlier exchange-rate depreciation, but should remain in the middle of the official target band (which falls from a range of $1\frac{1}{2}$ to $3\frac{1}{2}$ per cent in mid-1994 to 1 to 3 per cent by the end of 1995). The current-account deficit is projected to continue to narrow gradually, as a rising invisibles deficit partly offsets the widening trade surplus.

Table 5. **Short-term outlook**

Percentage changes, seasonally-adjusted annual rates, volume (1986 prices)

	1991 current prices C$ billion	1994	1995	1994 I	1994 II	1995 I	1995 II
Private consumption	412.2	3.1	3.2	3.6	3.1	3.2	3.4
Government consumption	144.4	−1.3	0.4	−2.2	0.0	0.5	0.7
Gross fixed investment	132.7	7.4	7.4	7.9	7.4	7.5	7.1
Public [1]	16.4	6.9	9.5	6.8	8.0	10.0	10.0
Private residential	39.8	4.8	6.4	6.7	7.0	6.5	5.8
Private non-residential	76.5	8.6	7.3	8.7	7.5	7.3	7.0
Final domestic demand	**689.4**	**3.1**	**3.6**	**3.3**	**3.4**	**3.6**	**3.7**
Change in stockbuilding [2]	−3.7	0.3	0.2	0.2	0.3	0.1	0.1
Total domestic demand	**685.7**	**3.3**	**3.7**	**3.5**	**3.7**	**3.7**	**3.8**
Exports of goods and services	163.9	10.0	9.1	10.3	10.4	9.0	8.2
Imports of goods and services	172.5	8.2	8.0	7.9	8.8	7.9	7.5
Change in foreign balance [2]	**−8.5**	**0.5**	**0.3**	**0.7**	**0.4**	**0.3**	**0.2**
Statistical discrepancy [2]	−2.4	0.2	0.0	0.4	0.0	0.0	0.0
GDP at market prices	**674.8**	**4.0**	**4.1**	**4.7**	**4.2**	**4.1**	**4.0**
Inflation							
GDP implicit price deflator		0.6	2.1	−0.2	1.6	2.3	2.2
Private consumption deflator		0.9	2.0	0.1	1.8	2.1	2.0
Unemployment rate [3]		**10.6**	**9.9**	**10.8**	**10.3**	**10.0**	**9.8**
Current balance (US$ billion)		**−21.7**	**−20.1**	**−22.0**	**−21.5**	**−20.4**	**−19.9**

1. Excluding nationalised industries and public corporations.
2. As a percentage of GDP in the previous period.
3. As a percentage of the labour force.
Source: OECD.

These projections, based on information available in September 1994, embody the following assumptions:

– with above-average growth projected for the United States in the near term, the expansion of Canada's export markets is expected to exceed that of world trade, averaging 8 per cent for manufactures (and somewhat less for total goods) over the next eighteen months or so;

– the average OECD crude-oil import price is assumed to rise from US$13.4 per barrel in the first half of 1994 to US$15 in the second half, remaining constant in real terms thereafter;

- assuming constant exchange rates, the rise in Canadian import prices is expected to slow to a rate of under 2 per cent in late 1995;
- given the budget-consolidation efforts at both the federal and provincial levels, the cyclically-adjusted general-government financial balance is projected to improve by around 1 per cent of GDP over the two years to 1995;
- with interest-rate differentials *vis-à-vis* the United States narrowing, Canadian short and long-term rates are expected to converge to 6½ per cent and 8 per cent, respectively, in late 1995.

The above projections are strongly dependent on growth performance in the United States, Canada's dominant export market. The strength of activity will also be determined by how quickly export demand can be translated into increased domestic employment and incomes. Given still high unemployment, consumer confidence may take time to recover, damping household spending. Confidence could also be adversely affected by a recurrence of financial-market disturbances. Indeed, foreign-investor concerns about the fiscal and political situation could limit the scope for a narrowing of interest-rate differentials – a central feature of the projections – thereby moderating the momentum of the recovery.

II. Economic policies

Overview

Over the past decade, the authorities have pursued a medium-term strategy aimed at reversing the deterioration in Canada's economic performance which began in the 1970s. Integrating both macroeconomic and microeconomic instruments, the policy approach has focused on reducing government deficits and inflation to create an environment conducive to sustained growth and on implementing structural reforms to promote the country's growth potential. As can be seen from Diagram 9, progress in achieving the strategy's objectives has been mixed, reflecting in part the time required for the private sector to adjust to the sweeping policy changes put in place (which included the Free Trade Agreement with the United States, tax reform and deregulation). While there has been a breakthrough in the inflation area – helped by the introduction of inflation-reduction targets – medium-term growth performance has continued to decline, and unemployment has remained on a rising trend. Moreover, despite a significant reduction in its structural component since the mid-1980s, the general government deficit has reached new peak levels in relation to GDP more recently, due to sluggish growth and an associated loss in tax revenues, leading to a marked increase in Canada's public debt.

The new Government that took office in late 1993 has assigned priority to reducing unemployment, and in particular its structural component (see labour-market section above). In this context, it has announced its intention to complete within two years a major reform of the unemployment-insurance system and other social programmes with the aim of loosening rigidities in labour markets and making those programmes financially viable (see Part III of the Survey). In keeping with the previous medium-term policy approach, the new Government has maintained – and extended until the end of 1998 – the inflation-control

34

Diagram 9. **INDICATORS OF ECONOMIC PERFORMANCE**

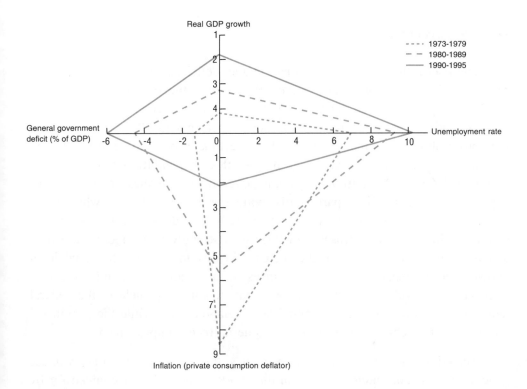

Source: OECD.

targets, while endorsing the goal of ultimately eliminating the federal budget deficit (an interim target of 3 per cent of GDP by 1996/97 was set to this effect). It has also continued to liberalise trade by signing the NAFTA and GATT agreements (see below).

The following paragraphs discuss in more detail the way the overall strategy has evolved and been implemented in recent years. Fiscal policy developments and the budget outlook are reviewed first; the conduct of monetary policy within the inflation-control-target framework is then examined, followed by an assessment of the progress in the structural-policy area.

35

The fiscal stance

General government

The rise in the general-government budget deficit has continued during the recovery, albeit at a much slower pace than during the recession of the early 1990s. As a proportion of GDP, the deficit on a national accounts basis widened from around 6½ per cent in 1991 to about 7 per cent in 1992, exceeding the previous peak recorded the mid-1980s. Latest estimates point to a further, though marginal, increase in 1993: although the growth of expenditures fell below that of nominal GDP (Diagram 10), general government revenues appear to have expanded even less. This is particularly evident at the federal level, where some tax rates were reduced, while some provinces bolstered their revenues through significant income-tax increases. Together with strongly rising federal transfers and better expenditure control, the increase in taxation at the provincial level allowed the aggregate deficit of provinces to start falling. But this was out-weighed by a widening federal government deficit. Nonetheless, the federal deficit is now lower than in the mid-1980s (Diagram 10), while the provinces' fiscal position is considerably weaker despite its recent improvement.

According to OECD Secretariat estimates, the renewed deterioration in the general-government budget balance in the 1990s is more than accounted for by cyclical factors: the "structural" (*i.e.* cyclically-adjusted) budget deficit appears to have declined further, reaching perhaps some 4½ per cent in 1993, although its downward trend has slowed sharply since the second half of the 1980s (Diagram 11). Despite substantial slippage from initial budget projections (see below), the stance of fiscal policy – as measured by the change in the cyclically adjusted budget balance – seems to have tightened in 1992, with a move towards restriction at the federal level more than offsetting the impact of expansionary provincial budgets. Roles were reversed in 1993, when fiscal tightening at the provincial level was accompanied by less restriction at the federal level, resulting in a slight easing of the overall fiscal stance. On announced policies, with generalised fiscal restraint, the decline in the structural deficit should resume in 1994-95. Combined with the positive effects of the economic upturn, this should make for a significant improvement in the general-government budget balance. However, at the present speed of budget consolidation, structural deficits are

Diagram 10. **BUDGETARY DEVELOPMENTS**
National Accounts Basis

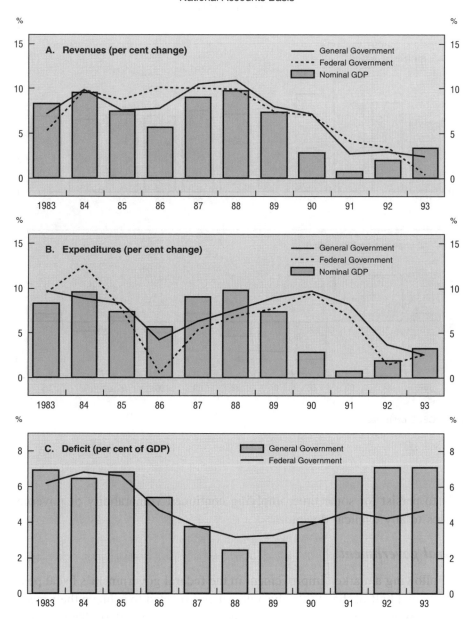

Source: CANSIM – Statistics Canada.

Diagram 11. **STRUCTURAL COMPONENT OF
THE GENERAL GOVERNMENT DEFICIT**
Per cent of trend GDP

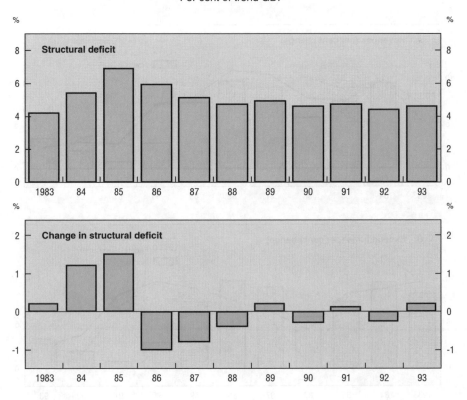

Source: OECD estimates.

likely to persist for some time, implying continued vulnerability of government finances to any cyclical downturn.

Federal government

Following a marked improvement in the federal government's fiscal position in the second half of the 1980s, the authorities expected to achieve their medium-term objective of a balanced budget by the middle of the 1990s. The slippage of deficits from budget projections was initially limited but became substantial in the last two fiscal years (ending in March, Table 6). Latest results for 1992/93 show, on a public accounts basis, a deficit of C$ 41 billion (6 per cent of GDP). This is some C$ 13 billion (2 percentage points of GDP) higher than envisaged in the February 1992 Budget. On the expenditure side, higher-than-projected transfers to provinces and Crown corporations were not fully offset by underspending in other areas. The revenue shortfalls reflect to a large extent lower-than-expected economic growth and inflation, which depressed tax receipts and unemployment-insurance contributions. However, revenues also dropped relative to nominal income, which was not expected, even taking account of discretionary policy actions (such as the restructuring of the child-benefit system and reductions in the personal-income surtax). Such a decline in the revenue-to-GDP ratio can in part be traced to tax refunds as a result of a lower-than-estimated tax base in preceding years.

At the time of the April 1993 Budget, the full extent of the deficit overrun in 1992/93 was not yet clear. Notwithstanding new initiatives to foster investment

Table 6. **Federal budget: projections and outcomes**

Public accounts basis; fiscal year (starting 1 April); per cent of GDP

	1992/93		1993/94			1994/95
	Budget	Outcome	Budget	Estimated outcome [1]	Outcome [2]	Budget
Revenues	18.5	17.5	17.7	16.1	16.3	16.8
of which:						
Taxes	17.1	16.0	16.2	14.8	15.0	15.7
Expenditures	22.3	23.4	22.2	22.5	22.2	22.1
of which:						
Programme spending	16.7	17.8	16.7	17.1	16.9	16.6
Public debt charges	5.6	5.6	5.5	5.4	5.3	5.5
Deficit	**3.8**	**6.0**	**4.5**	**6.4**	**5.9**	**5.4**
Memorandum items:						
Net public debt	62.6	67.7	68.3	71.9	71.4	74.5
Deficit excluding public debt charges	−1.8	0.4	−1.0	1.0	0.6	−0.1
Deficit on a national accounts basis	..	4.6	..	..	4.6	..

1. February 1994 Budget estimate.
2. September 1994 Annual Financial Report.
Source: Department of Finance, Statistics Canada.

and employment, fiscal restraint measures in other areas (notably a reduction in unemployment-insurance benefit rates) were considered sufficient to bring down the deficit to C$ 32.6 billion (4.5 per cent of GDP) in 1993/94. In the event, fiscal slippage continued. The February 1994 Budget put the 1993/94 deficit at C$ 45.7 billion (6.4 per cent of GDP). Although this estimate has proved to be too cautious, latest results still are for a deficit of C$ 42 billion, that is 5.9 per cent of GDP (Table 6). Helped by lower interest rates, expenditures were broadly in line with the 1993 Budget projections. Government revenues, on the other hand, declined sharply both in absolute terms and in relation to GDP. A number of one-time restructuring charges, as well as faster processing of refunds, lower quarterly personal income tax instalments and certain transitional costs relating to the introduction of the new child benefit system were the primary factors behind the decline in revenue. In addition, the new Government provided for certain liabilities (such as potential claims under the revenue stabilisation facility and expected costs for the cancellation of defence contracts).

The February 1994 Budget – the first introduced by the newly-elected Government – aims at reconciling initiatives for growth and job creation with steady reductions in the deficit. As for expenditures, restriction on civil service wages is extended and further cuts in unemployment benefits and defence spending are being implemented. Despite additional infrastructure investment and a number of measures to assist small and medium-sized businesses, federal government expenditure is projected to remain significantly below the ceilings set out in the previous Government's Spending Control Act. For that reason, no extension of the Act beyond the 1995/96 fiscal year is envisaged. The net impact of revenue-raising initiatives is minimal, with measures to broaden the tax base offset by lower unemployment-insurance contributions and tobacco taxes. Given the gradual implementation of some of the announced initiatives, net fiscal savings in the current fiscal year will be limited. The budgetary deficit for 1994/95 is estimated at C$ 39.7 billion (5.4 per cent of GDP). Adjusting for the non-recurring factors, which raised the deficit in 1993/94, this implies a decline by only about C$ 2½ billion. However, given the better-than-estimated outcome for the preceding fiscal year and cautious underlying growth assumptions, there is greater assurance that the 1994/95 deficit target will be met, despite the adverse effect of the recent rise in interest rates. Excluding debt charges, the budget balance seems set to move back into surplus (Table 6).

Contrary to previous years, the 1994 Budget does not include medium-term fiscal projections. Detailed estimates are only provided for 1995/96 when – with recent fiscal restraint measures taking their full effect and curbs on transfers to provinces (see below) – the budget deficit is expected to narrow to C$ 32.7 billion (4.2 per cent of GDP). This results from virtually flat non-interest spending (implying a marked decline in real terms), an only marginal increase in debt charges, and revenue growth slightly in excess of that of projected national income. In line with its election platform, the new Government is committed to reduce the budget deficit further to 3 per cent of GDP (around C$ 25 billion) in 1996/97. The achievement of this target is dependent on continued economic growth and lower interest rates than observed in mid-1994. If, for instance, interest rates remained at these levels, this would more than offset the incremental fiscal savings stemming from the 1994 Budget, requiring additional consolidation measures. While the Government's fiscal objectives are ambitious in so far as they would, within three years, bring down the deficit-to-GDP ratio to a level not achieved since the mid-1970s, they imply a further rise in the debt-to-GDP ratio (see below) which would peak in 1996/97.

Provincial governments

The rapid deterioration in the provinces' budget position in the early 1990s was a major factor behind the pronounced widening of the overall government deficit: in the three years to 1992/93 the provincial-sector deficit, on a public accounts basis, increased by 3 percentage points in relation to GDP, twice as much as the federal deficit, to reach 3.7 per cent (C$ 25.3 billion). The adverse financial-market reaction to these developments, as evidenced by numerous downgrades of provincial credit ratings, induced most governments (notably Ontario and Alberta) to take drastic restraint measures – both on the expenditure and revenue side – in their 1993 Budgets. In Ontario, the government imposed a freeze on discretionary spending, reduced drastically the civil service, cut health and education costs, and negotiated a "social contract" which reduced compensation to public employees in exchange for preserving their jobs. Except for Alberta, all provinces increased taxes. As a result, and with – contrary to the year before – relatively limited fiscal slippage, the provinces' deficit is estimated to have narrowed to C$ 20.3 billion (2.9 per cent of GDP) in 1993/94.

Progress in budget consolidation at the provincial level is likely to slow down, however, in the near term: in 1994/95, the provincial-sector deficit is projected to decline to C$ 17 billion (2.3 per cent of GDP). This is about C$ 3 billion ($\frac{1}{2}$ per cent of GDP) above the level envisaged a year ago. While most of the smaller provinces (and in particular Alberta) have again tabled very restrictive Budgets in recent months, the two largest provinces, Ontario and Quebec, whose governments face elections within the next year or so, have abstained from further important restraint initiatives. As a result, Ontario is set to replace Alberta as the province with the biggest per capita deficit while Quebec's relative deficit is likely to move above the provincial average (Table 7). If Budgets are implemented as planned, the two largest provinces' per capita deficit will be about five times as high as that of some of the smaller provinces, which are pursuing budget consolidation with more vigour. All smaller provinces envisage balancing their (overall or current account) budgets within three years – with Alberta and New Brunswick having passed balanced-budget legislation – while Quebec and Ontario expect to achieve this objective only towards the end of the decade. However, in most cases, additional measures of restriction are likely to be needed to meet the fiscal targets, not least because the 1994 federal Budget announced a freeze on some of the major transfers to provinces (for social

Table 7. **Per capita government deficits**

Canadian dollars

	1992/93	1993/94	1994/95
Ontario	1 210	902	804
Nova Scotia	844	764	651
Quebec	708	696	623
Alberta	1 305	926	571
New Brunswick	657	597	367
Newfoundland	461	387	342
Manitoba	509	411	262
British Columbia	531	380	261
Saskatchewan	587	290	184
Prince Edward Island	618	519	142
Provinces aggregated	**912**	**721**	**597**
Federal government	1 461	1 626	1 394
Total	**2 372**	**2 346**	**1 990**

Source: Toronto-Dominion Bank.

assistance and post-secondary education) in 1995/96, and their subsequent reduction to 1993/94 levels in 1996/97.

Debt developments

With persistent high budget deficits, public debt has continued to grow strongly. According to OECD estimates, on a national accounts basis, general government gross financial liabilities exceeded 92 per cent of GDP in 1993, more than twice the level recorded in the early 1980s, while net liabilities measured 62 per cent of GDP, as compared with around 10 per cent before the 1981-82 recession. Although similar trends can be observed in many other OECD countries, the gap between Canada and the OECD average has tended to widen (Diagram 12), reaching 24 and 22 per cent of GDP, respectively, for gross and net liabilities in 1993. Compared with the G7-economies, the differential was somewhat larger, with only Italy recording a higher debt ratio. In 1994, Canada's comparative debt position is likely to worsen further (Diagram 12).

The provinces' debt has increased by more than their budget deficits would suggest, because some governments have increasingly relied on off-budget spending, in particular on capital projects. The provincial share of total net government debt has risen from about one-tenth at the beginning of the 1980s to almost one-quarter more recently. Government debt has grown most quickly in Saskatchewan, Alberta and Quebec, the latter being now, in per-capita terms, the country's most indebted province.[5] Net per-capita debt is lowest in British Columbia and Alberta (despite the sharp deterioration in the debt position). While the foreign-currency debt exposure of the federal and local governments is low, that of the provinces is important: they now account for almost half of the total foreign-currency debt (of government, corporations and banks). With high and rising debt levels, seven provinces have seen their debt ratings cut further, over the past year, by at least one agency. Even the debt of some municipalities – whose average debt ratio is minor – and of the federal government have been downgraded, although in the latter case only the relatively limited foreign-currency debt has been affected. This has been reflected in sizeable credit premiums that governments must pay to finance their deficits.

These developments highlight the need for the early achievement of a sustainable fiscal position, allowing the stabilisation of the public debt-to-GDP ratio. As noted above, on current budget plans, the debt-to-GDP ratio would not

Diagram 12. **PUBLIC DEBT**[1]
As a percentage of GDP

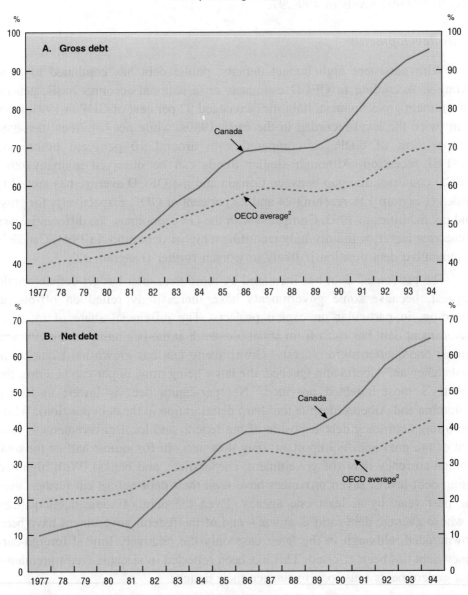

1. General government; national accounts definitions.
2. Weighted average of 17 countries (1987 GDP weights and exchange rates).
Source : OECD, *National Accounts;* Secretariat estimates.

peak before 1996/97, a time when the economic upturn would have lasted five years, and the risk of a cyclical downturn would be present. Given that the economy is now on a more favourable cyclical position than in many other countries where the recovery just started, more rapid progress in fiscal consolidation, with a view to improving the debt situation sooner than envisaged, would be appropriate.

Monetary management

The policy framework

Since 1991, monetary policy has been guided by inflation-reduction targets jointly announced by the Governor of the central bank and the Minister of Finance. Such a policy approach was adopted for four reasons:[6]

i) the authorities consider that the best contribution that monetary policy can make to improving economic performance is to achieve and maintain price stability;

ii) definite targets give households and businesses a clear indication of the inflation path that can be expected;

iii) they also provide a clear scale to measure monetary-policy performance; and

iv) given the loose link between other possible nominal anchors and prices, it seems preferable to use all available information to target the final objective (*i.e.* inflation) directly.

As can be seen from Diagram 13, this approach has been quite successful so far: initially falling below the target band, the annual increase in the consumer price index (CPI) has tended to run close to the lower end of the target range (*i.e.* 1.5 to 3.5 per cent by mid-1994), when adjusted for major changes in indirect taxes (notably the recent cuts in tobacco taxes). The fact that at times inflation has been lower than strictly prescribed by the targets reflects unexpected price shocks (in particular unusually low commodity prices). Indeed, it is the authorities' intention to respond symmetrically to pressures that threaten to drive inflation outside the target range. They have indicated, however, that overshooting targets is especially to be avoided during a period in which the central bank is attempting to reduce inflation and establish credibility.

Diagram 13. **INFLATION TARGETS**
Percentage change over 12 months

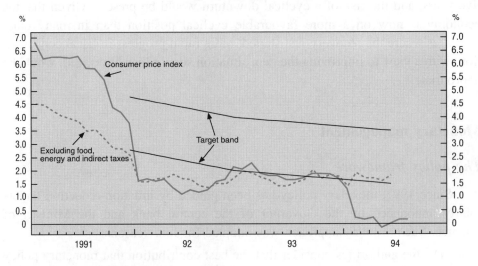

Source: CANSIM — Statistics Canada; Bank of Canada.

In December 1993, the new Government and the Bank of Canada reaffirmed the target of holding inflation inside a band of 1 to 3 per cent by the end of 1995, and agreed to extend it for three more years – when the "inflation-reduction" targets will become "inflation-control" targets. This implies a postponement of the achievement of the ultimate goal of price stability, previously defined for practical purposes as an inflation rate of "clearly below 2 per cent" after 1995.[7] But the authorities consider that more time is needed for the economy to adapt to a low-inflation environment, and for the Bank to gain experience in operating under these conditions, before a decision can be made on a target for the CPI that would be consistent with price stability.

The introduction of the inflation-reduction targets has not implied a fundamental change in the operation of monetary policy. The authorities have continued to base their policy decisions on a variety of financial and economic indicators, including monetary and credit aggregates, the exchange rate, wage developments, and capacity utilisation. However, because there may be a lag of six to eight quarters before policy actions have significant effects on the rate of

46

inflation,[8] projections and forward-looking indicators obviously play a greater role. The Bank staff explicitly works out a projected path for the interest rate that is consistent with the desired inflation rate given the quarterly forecasts for other key variables, in particular the output gap and the exchange rate, but is prepared to see offsetting movements between the exchange rate on the one hand and short-term interest rates on the other. Nonetheless, given the risk of snowballing movements and the potential disruptive effects of exchange-rate volatility – which often reflects *non*-monetary factors – the authorities have sought "to stabilise markets and to help them find viable trading ranges".[9] The key role of the exchange rate is highlighted by the fact that the Bank of Canada has focused increasingly on the weighted average of changes in short-term interest rates and in the effective exchange rate – a "monetary conditions index" – as a short-run operational target for policy.

Evolution of monetary conditions

As defined above, monetary conditions have eased substantially since the spring of 1990 – reflecting a downtrend in both short-term interest rates and (from 1992) the exchange rate (Diagram 14) – although from a very tight position. Moreover, the decline in interest rates was interrupted in the autumn of 1992, when a combination of external developments and domestic budgetary and political uncertainties led to severe downward pressure on the exchange-rate. As a result, monetary conditions tightened significantly during that period. But, as soon as this pressure on the dollar eased, the Bank resumed its accommodative stance, as evidenced by the substantial positive spread between money-market rates and overnight financing rates (Diagram 15). Except for a brief period – between the currency turmoil in Europe and the federal election in October – when the exchange-rate came under renewed pressure, short-term interest rates declined throughout 1993 and at the beginning of 1994, although the authorities intervened to dampen the fall in market rates in the latter part of this period.

By late January 1994, short-term interest rates had dropped to 3³/₄ per cent, the lowest level for thirty years. At the same time, the differential between Canadian and US short-term rates had narrowed to about 50 basis points, as compared with around 500 points in 1990 and in the autumn of 1992 (Diagram 15), and the chartered banks' prime lending rate had fallen to 5¹/₂ per cent, below the corresponding US rate. Thereafter, however – against the background

Diagram 14. **MONETARY CONDITIONS**

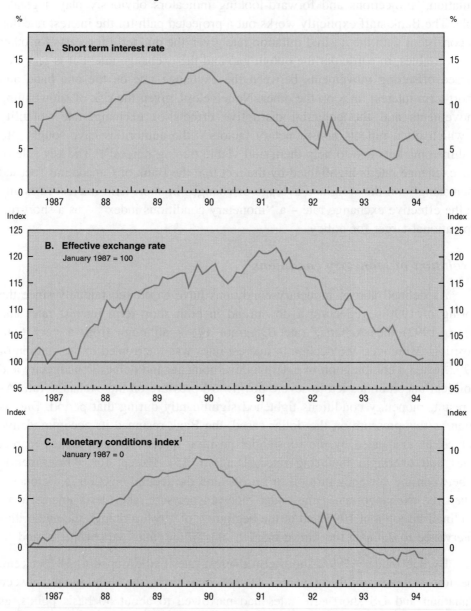

1. Index built by the Secretariat using a weighted average of changes in the interest rate (0.75) and in the effective exchange rate (0.25).
Source: OECD Secretariat.

Diagram 15. **INTEREST RATE AND EXCHANGE RATE DEVELOPMENTS**

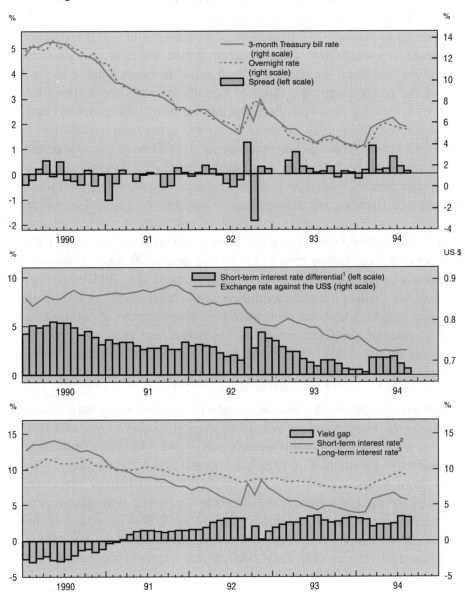

1. *Vis-à-vis* the United States.
2. 3-month corporate paper rate.
3. Over-10-year Government bond yield.
Source: CANSIM – Statistics Canada; OECD.

of concerns about Canadian governments' deficits and debts in the run-up to the February Budget as well as international markets that were unsettled by the US/Japan trade dispute – the tightening of monetary policy in the United States contributed to a weakening of the Canadian dollar, which in turn led to upward pressure on short-term interest rates. With price increases running at the lower edge of the target range, the Bank of Canada attempted to respond to these pressures by holding the overnight financing rate below money-market rates. For a while, interest differentials *vis-à-vis* the United States narrowed further. Subsequently, however, financial-market concerns over Canada's heavy public debt and the future of the federation resurfaced so that, with downward pressure on the currency intensifying, short-term interest rates rose sharply from mid-March. Although the Bank's cash management operations were aimed at helping the market find new trading ranges at higher interest rates, the overnight financing rate remained below 6 per cent while money-market rates fluctuated within the 6 to 7 per cent range during most of the second quarter. At times, Canadian short-term rates exceeded their US counterparts by more than 200 basis points. In response, the chartered banks raised their prime lending rate in several steps to 8 per cent in late June. Since then, with lessening concerns about the fiscal and political situation, the Canadian dollar has firmed and short-term interest rates have eased despite rising US rates, leading chartered banks to lower their prime lending rate to 7 per cent.

Long-term interest rates have also tended to decline, though to a lesser extent than short-term rates, resulting in a rather steep yield curve compared both with international developments and Canada's past experience. While financial-market disturbances in the autumn of 1992 left long-term rates largely unaffected, leading to sharp temporary narrowing of the yield gap (Diagram 15), during the recent episode these firmed almost as much as short rates, with government bond yields rising from a low of under 7 per cent in early 1994 to around 9½ per cent by June. Although the long-term interest-rate differential *vis-à-vis* the United States has tended to narrow since 1990, it has remained substantial, widening again sharply recently to reach temporarily around 200 basis points in mid-1994. This nominal differential has been particularly high in the light of the lower rates of inflation in Canada over the last few months. As can be seen from Diagram 16, the difference between Canada's long-term interest rate and current inflation is among the highest in the OECD area. In part this may have resulted from a more

Diagram 16. **REAL LONG TERM INTEREST RATES**[1]

1994 averages

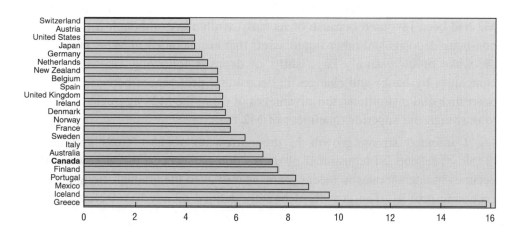

1. Governments bond yields less the current inflation rate.
Source: OECD.

gradual adjustment of long-term than short-term inflation expectations. But to a large extent the persistent substantial premium on Canada's long-term bonds would seem to be attributable to financial-market concerns about fiscal and political developments. While some of these concerns might have translated into fears about long-term future inflation (as evidenced by the differential between yields on nominal bonds and yields on real return bonds), there is little evidence that the recent increase in interest-rate differentials could reflect a rise in short-term inflation expectations.

Money and credit aggregates

Developments in monetary aggregates are characteristic of an economy about to experience an acceleration in the pace of economic expansion combined with low inflation. Over the past year, the Bank of Canada has increasingly focused on the monetary aggregates *gross* M1 and M2+ as leading indicators of activity and inflation rather than (net) M1 and M2, the previously preferred definitions of narrow and broad money. (Net) M1 had been thought to be a ''cleaner'' measure of transactions balances to the extent that it eliminated the possible double counting of payments in transit. But, in recent years, the estimated movements in private sector float[10] appear to have overstated the true impact of such payments on demand deposits, making (net) M1 more volatile. M2 had been favoured because of its early availability, although it excludes the non-bank deposits and other liquid assets that are included in M2+. However, in the wake of increasingly large shifts of deposits following takeovers of trust companies by banks and changes in depositors' preferences between banks and other financial institutions, the advantages of using the M2+ aggregate have come to outweigh the superior timeliness of M2.

Continued strong growth in the narrow aggregates gross and net M1 (Table 8) reflects an adjustment of transaction balances to the large cumulative declines in interest rates in recent years, as well as to the gradual strengthening of economic activity. The growth of broadly defined money has declined for four

Table 8. **Money and credit aggregates**

Percentage change

	1990	1991	1992	1993	1994 Q1	1994 Q2
					Seasonally adjusted[1]	
Monetary growth						
Gross M1[2]	0.8	2.2	6.1	9.2	28.7	7.3
Net M1[3]	–0.9	4.2	3.4	10.9	10.7	16.5
M2	11.0	6.8	3.7	3.2	0.5	–0.6
M3	10.3	6.4	5.2	4.9	–2.0	8.0
M2+	11.5	8.7	5.6	3.8	0.3	–0.6
Credit expansion						
To business sector	9.3	3.6	2.0	0.8	4.2	9.3
of which:						
Short term	7.3	0.4	–3.7	–5.3	–3.2	12.6
To household sector	12.5	6.7	6.3	5.8	8.0	9.3
Consumer credit	8.8	2.8	–0.1	1.5	12.0	6.3
Residential mortgages	14.1	8.3	8.9	7.3	6.7	10.5
Memorandum items:						
Nominal GDP growth	2.9	0.8	2.0	3.4	3.3	5.8
Income velocity (GDP/M1)	3.8	–3.3	–1.3	–6.7	–6.7	–9.2
Income velocity (GDP/M2)	–7.3	–5.6	–1.6	0.1	2.8	6.5
Income velocity (GDP/M3)	–6.7	–5.4	–3.0	–1.5	5.4	–2.0

1. Annual rate of change over preceding period.
2. Currency outside banks plus demand deposits.
3. Gross M1 minus private sector float, *i.e.* items in transit through the payment clearing system.
Source: Statistics Canada, OECD.

years in a row. For example, growth of M2+ fell to about 4 per cent in 1993 from double digits in 1989. This trend represents a movement towards a pace of monetary expansion more consistent with price stability, although part of the deceleration, especially in 1993, has been due to shifts by individuals and firms into mutual funds not included in conventional definitions of money. If previous empirical relationships continue to hold, monetary aggregate developments bode well for continued robust non-inflationary growth, since M2+ has been a useful indicator of inflationary pressures, while M1 has contained leading information about output growth.

Growth in private-sector credit moderated further in 1993 as a whole but has tended to strengthen since the second half of the year. Although the expansion of household credit slowed markedly from 1990 to 1993 (Table 8), it continued to exceed the growth in personal disposable income, causing the personal debt ratio to rise to a new high. This trend was supported by the decline in interest rates over that period, which has led to a sharp fall in the debt-service ratio. The recent revival in household credit growth was initially due to a rise in consumer credit associated with higher demand for durables, while mortgage growth continued to decelerate given sluggish housing market activity. However, in the spring of 1994, mortgage credit increased sharply, apparently because prospective homebuyers advanced house purchases to take advantage of preapproved mortgages at lower rates at a time when interest rates were firming. Business credit has also picked up since mid-1993, as rising profit margins, lower costs of funds and an improving sales outlook have boosted investment spending. Until early 1994, this reflected strong demand for longer-term sources of funds, with businesses taking advantage of lower long-term bond yields and buoyant equity markets to restructure their balance sheets. Since then, short-term business credit has expanded sharply, following a marked contraction since 1991 (Table 8). This may be the result of increased demand for working capital, although it is probably also related to a shift in financing away from bond and equity issues in the face of rising interest rates and a weakening stock market.

Structural reform

The numerous structural reforms implemented since the mid-1980s have focused on *i)* increasing opportunities for trade both internationally and domestically; *ii)* reforming the tax system; *iii)* enhancing public sector efficiency; and *iv)* reducing labour-market rigidities. The 1989 Free Trade Agreement (FTA) with the United States and the 1988-91 tax reforms, in particular, have been estimated to result in large gains in economic efficiency and potential output (up to 5 per cent), while the labour-market reforms launched in 1989 have been expected to lower the "natural" rate of unemployment significantly (see below). So far, there is little evidence that trend growth in total factor productivity has resumed, while the prolonged period of slack in Canadian labour markets appears to have raised structural unemployment, at least temporarily. As noted above, this probably reflects the difficulties for the economy to adjust to the important structural policy changes implemented in recent years, in the context of a reorientation of monetary policy towards controlling inflation and of insufficient fiscal consolidation. While substantial short-run costs have obviously been associated with these changes, benefits should arise in the longer term. However, there also appears to be scope for additional structural-policy action to boost potential output.

With a view to ensuring better growth and labour-market performance, the new Government is currently undertaking a number of comprehensive policy reviews, notably in the area of social security, support to small business, science and technology, transportation, customs tariffs and regulations, and indirect taxation. Reflecting the priority assigned to removing impediments to faster employment growth, the Government has already taken first measures to reform the unemployment-insurance system, enhance job training, support small businesses, promote technological innovation, and raise infrastructure investment.

Recent initiatives

Labour markets

In recent years, the government has implemented a number of reforms designed to reduce disincentives to take available jobs and to increase the skill level of the work force. The 1990 amendments to the Unemployment Insurance (UI) Act tightened the benefit structure and re-invested resulting savings towards active support for unemployed workers. Further modifications in 1993 included a reduction in UI benefit rate from 60 to 57 per cent of insurable earnings and tightening of eligibility requirements. Part of the savings generated by these initiatives has been allocated to financing experimental implementation of innovative approaches to assisting people and investing in human capital. The February 1994 Budget proposed further reforms along these lines, which became effective in July. As the first step of a broad overhaul of the income-security system (see Part III), the minimum period of work required to qualify for UI benefits was increased, the maximum duration of benefits reduced, and the benefit rate further lowered to 55 per cent (except for low-income beneficiaries with dependents); this will permit a rollback of the UI premium rate to the 1993 level from 1995. Assuming that only up to one-half of the people affected will be able to find work to cover for the lost benefits, the 1994 reforms are estimated to lower the "natural" rate of unemployment by 0.3 to 0.5 percentage points, somewhat more than the 1990 reform package.

Financial markets

Following the comprehensive reforms completed in mid-1992 – which dismantled many of the remaining barriers between federally-regulated financial institutions – the federal government has issued new regulations regarding the demutualisation of life-insurance companies, the establishment of specialised financing corporations, and the implementation of prudent portfolio rules for pension funds. Other recent regulatory developments include a comprehensive review of Canada's deposit insurance system, which is expected to cover early detection and intervention criteria, co-insurance, risk-based premiums, and asset valuation. The North American Free Trade Agreement (NAFTA, see below) includes provisions enhancing the ability of Canadian, American and Mexican financial institutions to participate in each others' financial markets.

Taxation

The new Government has identified as an immediate priority the reform of the Goods and Services Tax (GST), which was introduced in 1991. The main problems with the GST are: the complexity of having a value-added tax at the federal level and sales taxes at the provincial level; inconsistent product definitions resulting in similar products having different tax rates; the fact that small businesses view it as costly and difficult to handle; and tax evasion encouraged by the GST's unpopularity which partly reflects the fact that the GST is highly visible since it is levied at the consumer level while the federal sales tax it replaced was levied at the producer level. A parliamentary committee that was asked to draw up alternatives to the GST tabled its report in late June. It recommends replacing the GST with a National VAT; to make the tax less visible by including it in the retail price of goods and services; to simplify the accounting system for small business; to broaden the tax base and lower the tax rate; and to merge the ten different sales taxes now in place at the federal and provincial level while allowing for variable provincial rates. So far only Quebec has introduced a provincial sales tax modelled on the federal GST, and some provinces have immediately rejected the report's harmonisation proposal.

International and interprovincial trade

There have been five annual scheduled tariff reductions since the implementation of the FTA with the United States in 1989. A third, and final, round of accelerated tariff elimination covering about C$ 1 billion in bilateral trade, was negotiated and came into effect in 1993. From 1994, the North American Free Trade Agreement (NAFTA), including Mexico, effectively replaces the FTA. The NAFTA incorporates the basic elements of the FTA, as well as the provisions to protect cultural industries, social services, and supply-managed commodities. In addition to preserving and enhancing access to US markets gained under the FTA, it provides advances not present in the FTA in the areas of financial services, investment, and government procurement. Given the new Government's concerns with certain aspects of the NAFTA, supplemental agreements on labour and environmental standards have been negotiated, and agreement has been reached to initiate negotiations aimed at producing new rules governing dumping and subsidies by the end of 1995.

The successful conclusion to the Uruguay Round will also ensure greater access to foreign markets for Canadian goods and services (including grains, chemicals, wood, pulp, and paper) while reducing the import costs of Canadian firms. Researchers have estimated the gains for Canada at between 0.2 and 1.2 per cent of national income, as compared with estimated income gains in the 2.5 to 3.5 per cent range from the FTA. This relatively small impact of the Uruguay Round – similar to the estimated effect of the NAFTA – reflects the importance for Canada of bilateral trade with the United States, which has already been liberalised to a large extent. It must be noted, however, that many benefits of the Uruguay Round are not quantifiable. In other international trade matters, Canada is now undertaking a major review of its import regime with a view to making the tariff system simpler, transparent for users, and easier to administer.

As for interprovincial trade, the main areas of concern are the different provincial regulations governing commercial transportation, government procurement practices, restrictions on interprovincial trade in agriculture, and barriers to labour mobility created by differential provincial licensing and residency requirements for certain professions. Estimates of the cost of the 500 to 700 trade barriers vary widely, but their negative effects on resource allocation in the Canadian economy would seem to be substantial. Over the past year, a committee of federal and provincial trade ministers has negotiated a comprehensive Agreement on Internal Trade with a view of reducing impediments to the free flow of goods, services, capital and people in Canada. In mid-1994, governments agreed in principle to eliminate some interprovincial trade barriers, but many of the details still have to be worked out. The agreement includes a code of conduct on investment practices, a dispute-settlement mechanism, more open government procurement practices, and increased labour mobility between provinces. But a number of exemptions have been granted to some provinces, and the governments failed to agree on the sensitive issues of agriculture, food, alcoholic beverages, energy, and discriminatory procurement practices of provincial Crown corporations, leaving them to future negotiations.

Fisheries and agriculture

In 1992 and 1993, the government introduced programmes to assist fishermen and plant workers affected by the closure of the northern cod fishery and by subsequent groundfish declines in other regions. With the continued decrease in fish stocks necessitating an extension to the northern cod moratorium and restrictions to other fisheries, the Government has announced a new comprehensive five-year programme of adjustment and income support for an estimated 30 000 displaced Atlantic groundfish fishers and plant workers – The Atlantic Groundfish Strategy (TAGS). Federal funding for the TAGS, which will replace the expiring earlier programmes, totals C$ 1.9 billion over five years. The Strategy has two objectives: to restructure the fishery in Atlantic Canada through resource rebuilding and capacity reduction; and to make available meaningful opportunities for individuals concerned through adjustment programmes for older plant workers, training and literacy support, and a Youth Corps for people under 25.

By contrast, agricultural support has declined significantly in recent years, albeit from high levels. Latest estimates suggest that assistance to producers, as measured by the "producer subsidy equivalent" (PSE), fell from 45 per cent in 1991 to 32 per cent in 1993 – significantly below the OECD average (42 per cent) but still above the US level (23 per cent). Although this partly reflects the depreciation of the Canadian dollar over that period, government efforts to rationalise and reduce subsidy programmes – except the "safety net" ones – have played a major role. In co-operation with producers, governments have been working towards replacing commodity-specific price support measures with a "whole farm" income support programme, which from 1995 would cover all agricultural commodities except those under supply-management schemes (milk, poultrymeat and eggs). Under the Uruguay Round agreement, Canada will be able to continue to protect its supply-management industries, using tariffs and special safeguards rather than quantitative restrictions. Although minimum access commitments will have to be met, tariff equivalents will be high enough to restrict most imports, falling only slowly over the length of the agreement. On the other hand, the substantial grain transportation subsidies (paid to railways) will be phased out, or replaced, because they are no longer allowable under the Uruguay Round agreement.

Industrial policy

As noted above, the Government is undertaking policy reviews in the areas of support to small business and science and technology with the objective of redesigning programmes and making them more efficient. The issues being studied are financing, regulation and compliance costs, service delivery, and the re-engineering of support programmes in areas such as management skills, technology, innovation, and international trade. In the meantime, the Government is taking a number of initiatives to promote innovative activities in Canada, including support to the development of environmental technologies. The February 1994 Budget also announced several new industrial-policy programmes: the Canadian Investment Fund will work with private partners and the financial sector to identify the best way to provide long-term capital to innovative companies; the Business Networks Strategy will encourage co-operation among small businesses to help them achieve the size needed to compete in international markets; and the Canadian Technology Network will bring together small firms to design, and market globally, competitive products. In the area of transportation, commissions reviewing the reforms implemented in the second half of the 1980s have been supportive of further deregulation. The Government has launched consultations with stakeholders in order to reduce surface transportation subsidies or redirect them into new programmes that would improve efficiency. It is also investigating the commercialisation of some services, such as the Air Navigation System, and the introduction of competitive pricing. At this stage, it is difficult to judge the impact of these initiatives, which – in many cases – still have to be implemented.

Privatisation and public-sector reform

The Government has continued efforts to streamline the public sector and make its operation more efficient. In addition to the incremental cuts since 1992, further restraint on operating budgets has been imposed in the current fiscal year. Since 1992, more than 50 agencies and other government entities have been eliminated or consolidated, and the number of government departments has been reduced from 32 to 23. Forty Crown corporations (public enterprises) and government holdings have been privatised since the mid-1980s, contributing to a decline in employment by about 90 000 to around 120 000. The remaining 48 Crown corporations mostly represent small and/or unprofitable activities. While this limits the scope for further privatisation, the Government is examining case by case the possibility of divesting itself of investments no longer required as instruments of public policy.

Scope for further action

Although major structural reforms have already been implemented in recent years, there is room for additional initiatives in specific areas. In particular, as noted above, the Canadian internal market still has significant barriers to the free movement of goods, services, capital and labour, restricting competition across provinces and favouring inefficient producers. Numerous exemptions and areas yet to be negotiated are likely to make the recent intergovernmental Agreement on Internal Trade less comprehensive than originally intended. Hence, further progress towards reducing interprovincial trade barriers is of utmost importance.

To this end, signatories have committed to future negotiations to broaden and deepen the agreement. Moreover, despite a significant reduction in agricultural support in recent years, assistance is still higher than in the first half of the 1980s and a continued effort will be needed to keep subsidies on a downward trend. Also, the distortions associated with Canada's supply-management system for certain agricultural commodities remain, with high tariffs replacing import restrictions under the Uruguay Round agreement. Furthermore, despite recent labour-market reforms, disincentives to work embodied in federal and provincial income-support programmes are still a source of concern, as discussed in more detail in the following chapter.

III. The Canadian Income Security System

In Canada, as in many other OECD countries, the income security system constitutes a complex mixture of programmes which have evolved over several decades. The effects of two severe recessions (1981-82 and 1990-91), dislocation due to economic and technological change, as well as demographic and other changes in the nature of the labour force have resulted in a substantial increase in income security expenditure. These developments have raised concerns about the financial sustainability of the existing system, especially given that expenditures have remained stubbornly high during periods of improving labour market performance. Further concerns have arisen about several features of Canada's income security system, including evidence of a growing dependence on income support measures, a relatively heavy reliance on passive rather than active labour market programmes, and adverse incentives in several programmes which discourage participation in the labour force and investment in human capital formation. More generally, many observers question whether the current framework, whose key features were developed between the 1940s and 1970s, remains appropriate in the current economic and labour market environment. These concerns have prompted a comprehensive review by the federal government of the social safety net, as outlined in the February 1994 Budget documentation, with a view to implementing significant reforms in 1995-96.[11]

In presenting the background to these reforms, this chapter outlines the main features of, and problems associated with, the Canadian income security system, providing international comparisons where relevant. Particular attention is devoted to unemployment insurance and social assistance – the two programmes which form the core of the income security system and which provide an income "safety net" for most of the labour force of working age. The analysis focuses on both the costs and disincentive effects of the system; it also suggests directions for change to ensure that an adequate degree of income security is provided, while reducing employment disincentives and budgetary costs. It must be stressed, however, that the Canadian authorities are contemplating reforms that go well beyond the issues that are the main focus of what follows. The reforms envisaged encompass other forms of social security as well, like child support and federal assistance to post-secondary education. They are expected to treat income security as one element of a broader human-resource development strategy that has an overall focus on employability and learning as well as income security.

Despite the many problems highlighted in the following discussion, it is important to keep in mind the substantial benefits associated with comprehensive social insurance programmes. Unemployment insurance benefits, for example, have an important rationale in the sense that they partly relieve people who have lost their job from immediate financial concerns, thereby facilitating more efficient job-search. Likewise, related assistance benefits are a crucial element of any welfare system in the sense that they help reduce poverty among unemployed people, especially those traditionally viewed as unemployable, as well as provide a backstop for those in need who do not qualify for other forms of government assistance. These aspects are well illustrated by the findings of a recently published volume of studies examining labour markets and income maintenance programmes in Canada and the United States (Card and Freeman, 1993). This work concludes that Canadian labour market and income support policies mitigated against the 1980s trend of rising inequality that was prevalent in the United States.[12] However, this does not mean that the Canadian system is ideal. Instead, the system has important macroeconomic consequences, in as much as it raises the national rate of unemployment. Hence, over the longer term, improving the system could pay significant benefits.

Main features of the system

Structure

Canada's social security system consists of a large number of programmes delivered by federal, provincial and municipal governments. These programmes are of several types:[13]

- *social insurance programmes*, such as unemployment insurance, workers' compensation and the Canada and Quebec Pension Plans. These are financed in part by premiums paid by employers and employees and pay benefits to eligible participants in the event of outcomes such as unemployment, workplace injury or retirement;
- *income support programmes*, such as social assistance or welfare and the Guaranteed Income Supplement for seniors. These are not financed by premiums and are available in situations of established financial need;
- *demographic dependent programmes*, such as Old Age Security. These payments are made to certain categories of households, regardless of their financial position.

Canada also relies heavily on the income tax system to deliver social security assistance through the use of refundable tax credits where entitlement is based on family income, although these issues are not discussed directly in this chapter.

Table 9 summarises the main income security programmes and the related (direct) expenditures for 1993.[14] Income support to the elderly via the Canada and Quebec Pension Plans (CPP and QPP) and the federal Old Age Security (OAS) and Guaranteed Income Supplement (GIS) constitute approximately 40 per cent of these expenditures. Unemployment insurance and social assistance, the primary focus of this chapter, also account for a similar proportion of income security expenditures. Other programmes which account for more than 5 per cent of total income security expenditure include Workers' Compensation and the Child Tax Benefit (which in 1993 replaced the Family Allowances and non-refundable tax credits for children).[15]

Constitutional responsibility for such key aspects of social policy as welfare, social services, health and education rests with the provinces. However, the federal government plays a significant role in the funding of these programmes, with the administration being carried out by the provinces.[16] In the case of Unemployment Insurance (UI), a constitutional amendment provided the authority for the federal government to introduce this programme. As a result, both levels of government play major roles in the financing and administration of the Canadian income security system.

Table 9. Income security programmes and expenditures, 1993[1]

	Expenditures	Per cent of total
Programmes directed and funded by the federal government (subtotal)	**63 669**	**71.6**
Old age security (OAS)	14 421	
Guaranteed income supplement (GIS)	4 250	
Spouses' allowances (SPA)	434	
OAS/GIS/SPA (total)	19 106	21.5
Canada and Quebec pension plans[2]	17 156	19.3
Child tax credit[3]	2 325	2.6
Veterans' benefits	1 250	1.4
Family allowances[4]	2 186	2.5
Federal employment programmes and services	1 292	1.5
Unemployment insurance (total)	19 238	21.6
Unemployment	15 388	
Sickness	436	
Family related[5]	1 330	
Retirement	0	
Fishing	274	
Training[6]	1 568	
Work sharing	96	
Job creation	110	
Self employment	35	
Registered Indians: social assistance and social services	748	0.8
Vocational rehabilitation of disabled persons	364	0.4
Cost-shared programmes: Canada assistance plan (CAP, social assistance)[7]	**14 765**	**16.6**
Provincial programmes (subtotal)	**10 539**	**11.8**
Workers' compensation[3]	3 881	4.4
Tax credits and rebates	3 000	3.4
Other welfare programmes	2 600	2.9
Municipal social security[3, 8]	1 100	1.2
Total	**88 972**	**100.0**

1. Fiscal year ending 31 March, exceptions noted. All expenditures are in millions of dollars.
2. The CPP is directed by the federal government and the QPP by the Quebec government.
3. Calendar year data.
4. These are for the last three quarters of 1992 when the programme terminated.
5. Includes maternity, adoption and paternity benefits.
6. Includes training and supplementary allowance benefits, and course cost benefit payments.
7. Expenditures (CAP federal payments doubled) are under-reported due to a limit on the rate of increase of the federal contributions to Ontario, Alberta and British Columbia since 1990-91.
8. Excluding CAP cost-shareable expenditures.

Source: Social security statistics, Canada and Provinces, 1968-69 to 1992-93.

Objectives and form of unemployment insurance

The unemployment insurance programme dates from 1940, making it one of the oldest components of Canada's income security system. UI is also one of the largest income security programmes; even by international standards Canada devotes a relatively large proportion of GDP to unemployment compensation. As a result of its relative size and its many possible influences on economic and labour force behaviour, most proposals for reform of the income security system involve changes to the UI programme. This section provides an overview of the programme's objectives, main features, and behavioural impacts.

Historical evolution

The establishment of a public programme of unemployment insurance in Canada grew out of the experience of the Great Depression. The principle recommended by the Royal Commission on Dominion-Provincial Relations (the Rowell-Sirois Commission) – set up in 1937 to examine the division of powers between the federal and provincial governments – was that the federal government establish an insurance programme for unemployed employables, and that the provinces provide income support to unemployables.[17] The federal and provincial governments subsequently agreed to a constitutional amendment which gave the federal government authority to act in this area. The primary objective of the subsequently established UI programme was to provide insurance against the temporary loss of income associated with unemployment. Like other social insurance programmes, its rationale can be understood in terms of the failure of private insurance to protect against these risks.[18] Initially the design of the programme reflected the social insurance objective; for example, the programme was to operate on an actuarially sound basis, and coverage was limited to those with strong labour force attachments who faced a risk of unemployment.[19]

The UI programme has evolved significantly over time. Although the initial focus was on the insurance objective, numerous changes resulted in features with distributional, equity or other social objectives, which went beyond those of improving economic efficiency by correcting for market failure in private unemployment insurance. One example of change in this direction was the introduction of fishing benefits, covering workers in a highly seasonal industry for whom unemployment during the off-season is quite predictable. The regional differentiation of the programme (described below) can also be viewed as providing a

Table 10. **Unemployment Insurance regimes since the 1970s**

	1970 Programme	1971 UI Act	1981 Programme	1990 Reforms	1994 Reforms
	Replacement rate under different UI regimes (per cent)				
Regular	37-43	66 2/3	60	60	55
With Dependants	43-54	75	60	60	60*
	Number of weeks required to qualify for UI benefits				
Required number of weeks to qualify	At least 30 weeks of contributions to the programme in the last 104, with a minimum of 8 weeks in the last 52	8 weeks of insurable employment regardless of economic conditions	10 weeks with the regional unemployment rate above 9%, rising to a maximum of 14 weeks with the unemployment rate below 6%	10 weeks with the region's unemployment rate above 15%, rising to 20 weeks with the unemployment rate below 6%	12 weeks with the region's unemployment rate above 13%, rising to 20 weeks with the unemployment rate below 6%
	Determination of Number of benefit weeks				
	The duration of benefits is the lesser of 52 weeks or 50 per cent of the number of weeks of contribution in the last 104 weeks	Between 8 and 15 weeks of benefits entitled an unemployed individual to 8 weeks of benefits	One week of benefits payable for each week of employment, up to 25 weeks	20 weeks of work earned 17 weeks of benefits with 1 extra week for each week of work up to 25 weeks	One week of benefits for every 2 weeks of work, up to 40 weeks work. A second phase provides for an extra week for each week of work above 40 weeks up to 52 weeks of work
		Each additional week, up to 19, resulted in an extra week of benefits	One week of benefits for every additional two weeks of insurable employment over 25 weeks (maximum 13 weeks)	Every 2 additional weeks of work earned an extra week of benefits	An extra week for each week of work, up to 52 weeks of work
		For every 2 weeks of work above 19, an individual would be entitled to one week of benefits up to 18 weeks			

4 extra weeks were payable if the national unemployment rate was between 4 and 5%, and 8 extra weeks if the national rate exceeded 5%	2 extra weeks of benefits for every half percentage point by which the regional unemployment rate exceeded 4 per cent (maximum 32 weeks)	Each percentage point of the unemployment rate in excess of 6% earned about an additional 3 weeks of benefits	2 extra weeks of benefits for every percentage point of the regional unemployment rate in excess of 4%
6, 12, or 18 extra weeks of benefits were payable if the regional unemployment rate exceeded the national rate by 1-2%, 2-3% and more than 3%			
Overall maximum of 50 weeks	Overall maximum of 50 weeks	Overall maximum of 50 weeks	Overall maximum of 50 weeks

* Applies only to claimants with dependants *and* incomes less than half maximum insurable earnings.
Source: Statistics Canada.

mechanism for income support to workers in economically depressed regions. Other examples of broadening the goals of the programme include the introduction of special benefits for absences from work due to sickness, temporary disability, and the birth or adoption of a child, and the "clawback" of UI benefits received by high income recipients.[20]

Significant changes to the UI Act in 1971 made the programme more generous. In particular, they substantially increased its coverage, to virtually all paid workers,[21] reduced the amount of previous work needed to qualify for benefits, and raised benefits as well as their maximum duration. Special benefits for sickness, disability and maternity were also introduced at this time.

Since 1971, many of the changes to the UI Act have been in the direction of a more restrictive or less generous programme[22] (Table 10). For example, the single person benefit rate has been lowered in a series of steps from 67 per cent in 1971 (75 per cent for claimants with dependants and low earnings) to 60 per cent in 1978, to 57 per cent in 1993, and most recently (as part of the February 1994 Budget) to 55 per cent (or to 60 per cent for those with dependants and low earnings). Similarly, the minimum amount of work required to qualify for benefits, which was lowered from 30 to 8 weeks in 1971, was subsequently increased to between 10 and 14 weeks (depending on the regional unemployment rate, as described further below) in the late 1970s, to between 10 and 20 weeks in 1990 and to between 12 and 20 weeks in the most recent amendments. Other areas in which the UI programme has become more restrictive during the past two decades include provisions for repeat users, new entrants/re-entrants, and those who quit their job without just cause.

Despite these various amendments, UI expenditures and the number of beneficiaries have grown dramatically since the early 1970s. Diagram 17 shows UI benefit expenditures (in constant 1993 dollars) over the 1943-92 period, and the average weekly number of beneficiaries from 1976 (the earliest year for which such data are available). During the space of two decades real UI expenditures have increased approximately six-fold – from under C$ 3 billion in 1970 to between C$ 18 and C$ 20 billion in the early 1990s, while the average weekly number of beneficiaries has grown from approximately 700 000 in 1976 to approximately 1.4 million in 1991-92.

The increase in UI expenditures has taken place in a series of steps. Apart from the approximate doubling of real annual expenditures between 1971 and

Diagram 17. **UNEMPLOYMENT INSURANCE**[1]

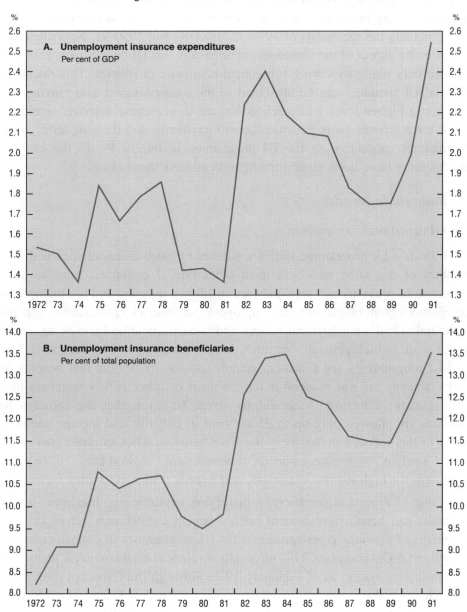

1. Beneficiaries with at least one dollar paid in a given year.
Source: Department of Human Resources Development, Canada.

1972 as the coverage of UI was greatly expanded and generosity enhanced, subsequent sharp increases were associated with downturns in economic activity – most notably the recessions of 1974-75, 1981-82 and 1990-91. Nevertheless, a disconcerting aspect of the Canadian experience is that UI benefit payments have declined only modestly during subsequent economic recoveries. This ratcheting effect of UI spending can be attributed to the unemployment rate moving to a persistently higher level with each downturn in economic activity, significant labour force growth, more generous benefit payments, and the long-term impact of structures introduced to the UI programme in the 1970s. In the last two decades there have been several attempts to address these issues.

Basic characteristics

• International comparison

Canada's UI programme shares a number of basic characteristics with programmes of the same nature in most other OECD countries. Benefits are a proportion of previous earnings, they are of limited duration and are financed by contributions from employers and employees (see below). Qualification depends on the individual's employment history and is conditional on them being available for work (which generally requires that a ''suitable job'' be accepted). Like most UI programmes, the Canadian system also has the feature that benefits for most claimants are not reduced if the claimant or other family members have other sources of income. It should be noted, however, that the earnings for claimants are allowed only up to 25 per cent of benefits, and income earned in excess of this reduced dollar for dollar from benefits. Also, as noted previously, in the Canadian programme a portion of benefits are ''clawed back'' through the tax system for high income claimants, and benefit generosity varies regionally.

Table 11 reports information on qualifying requirements, maximum benefit durations, and benefit replacement rates – benefit entitlements before tax as a percentage of previous gross earnings – for UI programmes in Canada compared with other OECD countries. This information refers to each country's unemployment insurance system as of 1 January 1989, although the Canadian programme has undergone three sets of amendments since then. For Canada therefore the current regulations (*i.e.* those proposed in the February 1994 Budget) are also shown. The ''reference period'' is the period of prior work history over which benefit entitlement is calculated; ''maximum benefit duration'' refers to the maximum length of time benefits can be received; and the "employment record" represents the minimum amount of employment during the reference period which is required to qualify for the maximum duration of benefits.

In this comparison, the Canadian UI system does not stand out in terms of the replacement rate, the length of the reference period, or the maximum benefit duration. The 55 per cent replacement rate is in the middle of the OECD range, and many other OECD countries have a one year reference period and maximum benefit duration of approximately one year. However, Canada (in the high employment regions), the United Kingdom and Sweden are somewhat unique in providing benefits for up to 50 to 60 weeks to those qualifying for UI on the basis of relatively brief employment spells (11 to 20 weeks). This feature was significantly altered by the 1994 changes to the UI Act. Nonetheless, it remains the case that in Canada's high-unemployment regions relatively brief periods of employment qualify individuals for relatively long periods of benefit eligibility.[23]

Nevertheless, caution must be taken when using international comparisons of replacement rates since, in practice, they are likely to be significantly different than those displayed in Table 11 given that they do not account for all of the relevant factors. In the case of Canada, the actual replacement rates would change if provincial governments' means-tested social assistance payments for individual unemployed people and their families whose UI benefit payments had run out were included. The data also do not account for: tax-relief opportunities for the unemployed; certain benefits such as housing assistance; those individuals who have only a short history of work or no record at all; and eligibility conditions such as the period an individual must wait to be eligible for a benefit when becoming voluntarily unemployed.

• Regional variations

Regional differentiation has been an important feature of Canada's UI programme since 1971. Both the length of the qualifying period (the minimum number of weeks of insured employment required to qualify for benefits) and the maximum duration of benefits depend on the unemployment rate in the UI region in which the individual files a claim. There are currently 62 UI assistance regions which, with the exception of Prince Edward Island, are much smaller than provinces. Essentially, the maximum benefit duration has two components, one based on the claimant's work experience during the qualifying period (the

71

Table 11. The rate and maximum duration of insurance benefits
Prime-age unemployed worker[1]

	Qualifying conditions and maximum duration of benefits[2]			Initial relation to earnings[3]		Initial gross replacement rate at average production worker levels of 1988 earnings[4]		
	Reference period (years)	Employment record (weeks)	Maximum benefit duration (months)	Formula	Per cent replacement rate	Single	With spouse	
							At work	Dependent
European community								
Belgium	2¼	90	Indefinite	P	60	60	60	60
Denmark	3	..[5]	30	P	90	64	64	64
France	2	52	30	L	–	59	59	59
Germany	4	156	12	P	63[6]	58	58	58
Greece	1	28	5	P	50	50	50	50
Ireland	1	48	15	L	–	29	29	43
Italy	1	104	6	P	15	15	15	15
Netherlands	5	156	36	P	70	70	70	70
Portugal	..[7]	..[7]	..[7]	P	60	60	60	70
Spain	4	192	24	P	80	62	62	80
United Kingdom	1	..[8]	12	F	–	16	16	26
Other OECD Europe								
Austria	5	156	7.5	L	–	41	41	44
Finland	4	..[5]	24	L	–	59	59	59
Norway	2	..[5]	20	P	62	62	62	62
Sweden	1	60	15	P	90	90	90	90
Switzerland	2	72	12.5	P	80	70	70	70
OECD non-Europe								
Japan	1	24	7.5	L	–	48	48	48
United States	1	20[8]	9	P	50	50	50	50
Canada, 1989[9]								
Maximum entitlement region	1	21	11.5	P	60	60	60	60
Minimum entitlement region	1	52	8.75	P	60	60	60	60

72

Canada, 1994 [10]

Maximum entitlement region	1	49	12.5	P	55	55	55
Minimum entitlement region	1	52	9	P	55	55	55

1. This is a simplified version of Table 7.A.1. in OECD (1991). See Annex 7.A. of that publication for further details of the definitions. The table refers to the system on 1 January 1989 and to a worker 40 years and 1 day old (except in a few countries, the same rates apply at other ages between 25 and 50 or 55). Changes to the UI system have subsequently taken place in some countries. For the United States, actual provisions vary by state (an approximately representative case is shown). The married person cases refer to a couple without children and provisions for couples with children may be different.

2. To qualify for the maximum duration of insurance benefits, the worker must have had the employment record listed during the reference period, counting the reference period up to the time of entering unemployment (except in Denmark, Finland and Norway, see note 5 below).

3. Initial relation to earnings. Formula: P = proportional; L = linear; F = fixed. Rate: benefit as per cent of previous earnings, shown only where the formula is proportional. The rate shown is for a single person. See Table 7.A.1 in OECD (1991) for details of how benefits in some countries fall during a prolonged spell of unemployment.

4. See the preceding note. This replacement rate refers to benefits before tax as a percentage of previous earnings also before tax, when the unemployed person before entry to unemployment and the spouse in work have 1988 Average Production Worker (APW) level of earnings. The gross replacement rate can be less than the percentage rate of benefit when there is a ceiling to insurable earnings that is below the APW level.

5. Denmark, Finland and Norway use or used (this has recently changed in Norway) a rolling reference period: for any period of this length, the maximum duration of benefits cannot be exceeded. Some employment or earnings record is also required.

6. In Germany, exceptionally, benefits are shown here as a proportion of earnings after tax and social security contributions (because the benefit rules take this form). Replacement rates take account of the fact that 13th month earnings do not enter the reference wage.

7. In Portugal, before recent reforms the entire record of past earnings could be taken into account if the worker could prove past employment by producing pay slips. A person producing 10 years of pay slips qualified for 13 months' insurance benefit.

8. In the United Kingdom, a certain level of insurance contributions is needed to qualify for insurance benefits. About 71 weeks of work at the APW earnings level are needed to qualify, more weeks with lower earnings. Many states in the United States also refer to the earnings record for UI.

9. Maximum and minimum entitlement regions refer to regions with unemployment rates more than 11.5 and less than 4 per cent respectively.

10. Maximum and minimum entitlement regions refer to regions with unemployment rates more than 16 and less than 6 per cent respectively.

Source: See OECD (1991, Annex 7.A).

52 weeks prior to the claim) and one based on the unemployment rate in the UI region. These features have two potentially important consequences. One is that in an economic downturn the maximum duration of UI benefits increases in most regions of the country. This consequence has been particularly relevant since 1977/78 when the maximum benefit duration was made a function of the regional unemployment rate rather than a function of the difference between the regional unemployment rate and the national unemployment rate, as was the case during the 1971-76 period.

Another consequence of the regional differentiation of the programme is that in high-unemployment regions there is a substantial economic return associated with relatively brief periods of employment. For example, under the UI provisions introduced in the late 1970s, 10 weeks of employment entitled a claimant in a high-unemployment region to 42 weeks of benefits.[24] By changing both the minimum qualifying period and the maximum benefit duration, recent amendments to the UI programme (particularly those introduced in the February 1994 Budget) have substantially reduced the return from brief employment spells. Nonetheless, this remains a distinctive characteristic of the Canadian system. For example, under the current regulations, 12 weeks of employment entitles an individual in a high-unemployment region (regions with an unemployment rate in excess of 16 per cent) to up to 32 weeks of benefits. However, at present less than 5 per cent of Canada's labour force is in such regions.

• Active labour market measures

The UI Act allows expenditures for "developmental uses" in cases where the normal provision of benefits to support job search may not be the most effective approach. Training, worksharing, job creation and, most recently, self-employment assistance benefits are funded under this provision of the Act. These programmes have typically accounted for a small proportion of total UI spending. However, since the changes introduced in 1990, funding for UI-sponsored training has increased substantially – from under C$ 300 million in 1989 to C$ 2.2 billion in 1993. As part of this increased emphasis on training and related active measures, the Labour Force Development Board was created in 1991 to provide a mechanism for private sector involvement in UI-sponsored training and other developmental programmes. The Labour Force Development Board is specifically involved in the management and direction of these programmes.

• Financing

The UI programme is financed in full by contributions from employers and employees.[25] Contributions are kept in a UI account, which should balance over a "cycle", but which can be in a cumulative deficit/surplus at any point in time. In this manner, the UI account should act as a stabiliser, at least in the first one or two years after any shock. However, there is some discretion on the part of the federal government as to the size of imbalances allowed in the account. A "statutory" contribution rate is formally calculated based on what rate balances the account over a moving three-year period. This may impose either a floor or ceiling on the contribution rate. The final decision is made jointly by the Ministry of Finance and the Department of Human Resources Development.

Contributions are proportional to insured earnings, subject to a ceiling. As is the case in most OECD countries, UI premiums are not experience-rated: they are independent of layoff rates (in the case of employers) and extent of UI receipt (in the case of employees).[26] Thus, there is cross-subsidisation between firms and industries with high layoff rates and those with stable employment patterns. In contrast to the Canadian and European UI programmes, most United States programmes are experience-rated, although the degree varies by state and is generally less than 100 per cent. Table 12 shows the behaviour of UI premiums over the past decade. Although premiums were lowered during the 1985-88 period, they have subsequently risen sharply – by over 50 per cent since 1989, partly explained by a major policy shift whereby funding of the programme was shifted entirely to employers and employees. Despite these steep increases,

Table 12. **Unemployment Insurance premiums, 1985-94**

Year	Contribution per C$ 100 of insured earnings	
	Employee	Employer
1985	2.35	3.29
1989	1.95	2.73
1990	2.25	3.15
1991 January to June	2.25	3.15
1991 June to December	2.80	3.92
1992	3.00	4.20
1994	3.07	4.30

Source: Human Resources Development, Canada.

75

the UI Account ended 1993 with a cumulative deficit of approximately C$ 6 billion. The deficit is, however, expected to fall sharply, so that the account will be in surplus by 1996.

Objectives and form of social assistance

Canada's social assistance programmes have been cost-shared in a comprehensive manner between the federal and provincial governments since the introduction of the Canada Assistance Plan (CAP) in 1966.[27] Predecessor programmes were categorical in nature, providing means-tested benefits to specific clientele such as the blind, disabled, aged, unemployed, and they were funded under a different federal-provincial formula. Benefits are available to anyone who is in need of assistance, which is based on a means test on family income and assets. Benefit levels, eligibility provisions, and other regulations vary by province and, in some cases, at the local level. The programmes are administered at the provincial and, in some cases, the municipal level. However, virtually all operate under the provisions of the Canada Assistance Plan. The federal government fully finances social assistance for registered Indians on reserve.

The basic features of the Canadian social assistance programmes are similar to those in many other OECD countries. Social assistance benefits do not depend on previous employment and are unrelated to past earnings; they are generally of unlimited duration and subject to a means test based on family wealth and income. Families with financial or non-financial assets are required to run them down to a bare minimum of personal effects before receiving social assistance. The universal nature of Canadian social assistance contrasts with that of the United States where welfare is largely restricted to single mothers with children. Canadian benefit levels are also much higher than their United States counterparts.[28] In these respects (universality of coverage, benefit levels), Canadian social assistance programmes are closer to their counterparts in many European countries. An important difference, however, between Canada and several European countries is that unemployment insurance and unemployment assistance programmes are not integrated as they are in several European countries.

The federal, provincial and municipal governments also provide a wide range of social services. These include: home support or counselling services for people with disabilities; protection for children subject to abuse or neglect; assistance to women and children who are victims of family violence; and assistance to low-income parents who need subsidised day care in order to participate in the labour force. As with social assistance, these services are also largely provided on a cost-shared basis under CAP. Table 13 provides the composition of the federal government's 7.3 billion FY 1992/93 transfer to the provinces under this programme.

Diagram 18 shows expenditures on total social services[29] over the 1963 to 1993 period as a proportion of GDP.[30] Following the introduction of the CAP, annual expenditures grew steadily until 1977, with a particularly large increase occurring between 1968 and 1973. From 1977 to 1981 annual real expenditures remained approximately constant. The 1981-82 and 1990-91 recessions again resulted in large increases in spending. However, an important question is why real social assistance expenditures did not decline (indeed, generally continued to rise) during 1985-89, a period which was characterised by strong economic growth. Although by 1989 the national unemployment rate had returned to its level of 7.5 per cent recorded before the 1981-82 recession, social assistance spending was still approximately 50 per cent higher in real terms.

As shown in Diagram 19, the number of welfare recipients has grown from 1.2 million in 1968 (almost 6 per cent of the population) to approximately 3 million in 1993 (over 10 per cent of the population). Substantial increases in the number of recipients are evident in the periods of economic downturns (i.e. between 1970-71, 1974-75, 1981-82 and 1990-91). However, throughout the long period of economic growth following the 1981-82 recession, the number of welfare recipients declined only modestly and did not return to its pre-recession level.

Table 14 presents selected CAP-related statistics by province for 1990/91. Quebec is the highest per capita recipient, with Ontario second. However, Ontario has the highest proportion of social welfare recipients and by far the fastest growth rate in per capita expenditure during the 1980s. This reflects both the growth in the number of recipients but also a significant increase in the generosity of programmes. Table 14 also shows provincial comparisons of benefit levels for single parent/one child families. These include basic social assistance, family allowances, the child tax credit, other child related benefits, sales tax/GST credits, provincial tax credits, and various other benefits in some provinces. The benefit levels vary significantly across provinces, with Ontario the most generous and almost the only province to experience growth in real terms over the 1980s.

Table 13. **Breakdown of social expenditures**[1]

	Per cent
Social assistance	62
Welfare service administration	8
Subsidised child care	4
Counselling and rehabilitation	4
Residential care	7
Health care	5
Child welfare	5
Homemaker	2
Other	3
Total	100

1. 1992/93 fiscal year.
Source: Human Resources Development, Canada (1994*b*).

Diagram 18. **TOTAL SOCIAL SECURITY EXPENDITURE**[1]
Per cent of GDP

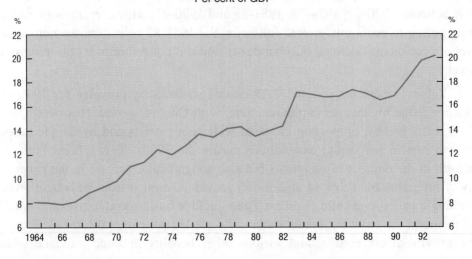

1. Includes health expenditures.
Source: Social Security Statistics, Department of Human Resources Development, Canada.

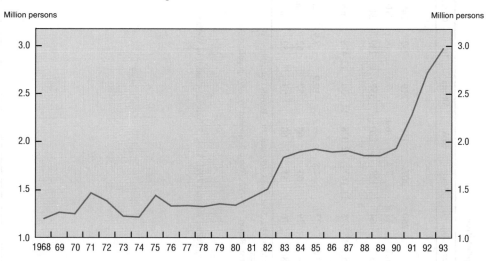

Diagram 19. **WELFARE RECIPIENTS**[1]

1. Includes claimant plus all dependents.
Source: Department of Human Resources Development, Canada.

In contrast, Quebec has the second lowest benefit level. Moreover, the Table compares the benefit levels to the low income cut offs (LICOs) estimated by Statistics Canada. These are levels of income (adjusted by community and family size) at which it is estimated that households spend more than approximately 55 per cent of their income on food, clothing and shelter. Individuals' benefits obviously fall well short of the LICOs in all provinces. However, a problem with using LICOs is that they measure relative poverty rather than absolute poverty and result in the poverty line rising with general living standards.

Comprehensive national data on the characteristics of the social assistance population are not available. However, as an illustration not necessarily relevant for the whole of Canada, Table 15 shows the composition of social assistance caseload for the province of British Columbia over the 1980-92 period.[31] Single men and women make up more than half of those on welfare. The rise in the proportion of the caseload accounted for by this group (from 57 per cent in 1980-82 to 64 per cent in 1991-92) is due to the increasing proportion of cases

79

Table 14. **Social assistance by province**

	NFLD[1]	PEI	NS	NB	Quebec	Ontario	Man.	Sask.	Alberta	BC	Canada
1. CAP Transfers[2] per capita 1990/91 (C$)	207	219	210	239	278	250	207	159	219	232	245
2. Assistance Recipients per capita[3] (%)	10.5	9.0	10.3	10.8	10.2	11.9	7.4	6.1	7.5	8.7	10.1
3. CAP growth 1980/81 -1990/91 (%)	226	231	312	221	223	464	328	220	357	239	244
4. Welfare benefits, 1991 single parent, one child[4] (C$)	12 347	12 343	11 961	9 841	10 975	16 098	11 167	12 028	11 630	12 478	n.a.
5. Growth rate of 4 (real terms), 1986-91[5] (%)	-1.2	-3.3	1.0	-6.0	-7.8	+23.6	-4.8	-6.9	-10.9	8.9	n.a.
6. Row 4 as percent of LICO[6]	69	71	67	55	54	79	55	68	57	62	n.a.
7. Row 4 as percent of average income[7]	67	–	59	53	48	70	55	60	53	52	n.a.

1. NFLD: Newfoundland, PEI: Prince Edward Island, NS: Novia Scotia, NB: New Brunswick, Man.: Manitoba, Sask.: Saskatchewan, BC: British Columbia.
2. CAP Annual Report; 1991-92, Table 7, divided by 1990 population. CAP is Canada Assistance Plan.
3. Number of persons assisted under the Canada Assistance Plan, as of March, 1992. From CAP Annual Report, 1991/92 , Table 2, divided by 1991 population.
4. From Welfare Incomes 1991, National Council of Welfare, Table 1.
5. This is a five-year growth rate. Welfare Incomes 1991, Table 4, National Council of Welfare.
6. LICO is Statistics Canada Low-Income-Cut-Off rate for a single parent with one child (1991).
7. Average income is defined as the average income of female single parents in the workforce. Source: Welfare Incomes 1991, Table 3, National Council of Welfare.
Source: Courchene (1994).

Table 15. **Per cent of social assistance spells by year in British Columbia**

	1980-82	1983-84	1985-86	1987-88	1989-90	1991-92
Type of claimant:						
Employable	38.4	54.2	56.1	52.1	58.5	63.8
Unemployable	61.5	45.8	43.9	48.0	41.6	36.2
Type of household:						
Couple	14.2	15.8	14.3	12.7	11.2	10.8
with children	7.9	10.2	9.2	8.0	6.7	6.7
without children	6.3	5.6	5.0	4.7	4.5	4.1
Single female	50.9	43.2	43.5	46.7	48.7	45.5
with children	27.4	21.7	22.3	24.9	25.7	23.4
without children	23.5	21.5	21.2	21.8	23.0	22.1
Single male	34.0	41.1	42.3	40.6	40.1	43.7
with children	1.0	1.3	1.4	1.4	1.3	1.5
without children	33.1	39.8	40.9	39.2	38.8	42.2
Age:						
Less than 21 years	14.4	15.9	13.7	12.2	12.3	12.9
21 to 25 years	14.1	16.3	15.8	14.3	12.8	13.5
26 to 36 years	27.4	29.7	30.8	31.8	31.9	32.6
Over 36	44.1	38.1	39.7	41.8	43.1	41.1

Source: Cragg (1994).

who are single men (this rose from 33 per cent in 1980-82 to 42 per cent in 1991-92). Single parents with children account for about 25 per cent of the caseload and couples 10 to 15 per cent. The age structure of the social assistance population in British Columbia has changed little over the past decade. About 25 to 30 per cent of welfare recipients are under 26 years of age.

Although single parents with children make up only 25 per cent of welfare recipients in British Columbia, they experience longer social assistance spells and thus account for much more than one-quarter of expenditure. The British Columbia data also indicate that there is substantial movement on and off social assistance. About three-quarters of all welfare spells lasted less than six months; just over 10 per cent lasted more than one year. Half of the spells experienced by singles, couples, and single parent families ended within four, three and six months respectively. However, there is a substantial amount of repeat use; over the 1980-92 period only one-third of the spells were the first spell for that individual or family.

Problems associated with the system

Rising expenditures

Direct expenditures on major income security programmes have displayed substantial growth since the early 1960s, albeit not all at the same rate nor at a steady pace (Table 16). A significant amount of the expenditure growth can be attributed to the fact that, as discussed above, programmes were introduced or broadened in scope during the 1960-75 period.[32] Income security expenditures constituted about 3 per cent of GDP during the 1960s and early 1970s, rising to around 5 per cent of GDP by the late 1970s. However, although the major programmes were already in place, following the 1981-82 recession and subsequently, expenditures on income security have exceeded 10 per cent of GDP.

Table 17 shows total social security expenditures (defined as income security plus health programmes) after adjusting for inflation and relative to various measures of growth of the economy and population. By any scale, real expenditures on social programmes have risen substantially. Between 1958-59 and 1980-81, real social security spending increased five-fold, followed by a further 60 per cent increase during the 1980s. In per capita terms, real expenditures increased by over 250 per cent between 1958-59 and 1980-81, and a further 45 per cent during the 1980s. Social programme spending also more than doubled as a percent of GDP and accounted for a greater share of total government expenditure (including debt financing) during this period. This rising cost of social programmes is obviously a matter of urgent policy concern.

Furthermore, as noted above, the rise in UI spending has resulted in substantial increases in premiums paid by employers and employees, and payroll taxes to finance other social security programmes have also risen substantially in recent years. The recent C$ 2.4 billion reduction in UI will, however, lead to lower premium rates in 1995 and 1996. Nevertheless, at a time when one of the greatest economic challenges is job creation, significant increases in the cost of labour have thus been taking place – especially relative to the cost of capital (Diagram 20) – augmented by the rising cost of income security programmes.[33]

Nevertheless, Canada is by no means unique in experiencing sharp increases in social spending. During the 1960s and 1970s, the majority of OECD countries faced similar pressures. During the early 1980s and 1990s the presence of weak economic growth further increased expenditure on income security programmes.

Table 16. **Canadian income security expenditures by major programmes**[1]

	1963-64	1968-69	1973-74	1978-79	1983-84	1984-85	1985-86
Family allowances and child tax credit[2]	538	633	1 011	2 967	3 774	3 912	3 985
OAS/GIS/SPA	808	1 541	3 034	5 491	10 406	11 418	12 525
Training and employment programmes[3]	0	108	191	201	247	274	1 465
Registered Indians' programmes[4]	0	30	68	135	275	303	337
Veterans' programmes[5]	256	319	403	674	1 079	1 133	1 151
CPP/QPP	0	30	385	1 801	4 938	5 852	6 787
Unemployment insurance	366	459	2 028	4 475	9 932	10 170	10 128
Workers' compensation	109	172	330	798	1 801	2 041	2 266
Cost-shared social assistance and social services	341	800	1 617	3 469	7 449	8 241	8 717
Provincial and local welfare programmes	188	243	739	2 387	4 295	4 349	4 607
Total income security	**2 607**	**4 336**	**9 866**	**22 397**	**44 195**	**47 694**	**51 966**
Total income security as a per cent of GDP	**5.34**	**5.60**	**7.4**	**8.99**	**10.61**	**10.53**	**10.69**

	1986-87	1987-88	1988-89	1989-90	1990-91	1991-92	1992-93
Family allowances and child tax credit[2]	4 107	4 203	4 572	4 717	4 845	5 146	4 511
OAS/GIS/SPA	13 444	14 349	15 202	16 152	17 130	18 392	19 104
Training and employment programmes[3]	1 560	1 528	1 509	1 562	1 568	1 423	1 292
Registered Indians' programmes[4]	371	420	477	529	633	691	748
Veterans' programmes[5]	1 154	1 164	1 142	1 162	1 199	1 217	1 251
CPP/QPP	7 853	9 735	11 113	12 429	13 802	15 389	17 153
Unemployment insurance	10 639	10 577	10 976	11 816	14 467	18 434	19 238
Workers' compensation	2 589	2 798	2 816	3 044	3 495	3 735	3 881
Cost-shared social assistance and social services	9 056	9 639	10 410	11 218	13 426	13 903	15 130
Provincial and local welfare programmes	4 423	4 568	4 877	5 699	6 312	6 657	6 657
Total income security	**55 198**	**58 854**	**63 104**	**68 335**	**76 885**	**84 994**	**88 972**
Total income security as a per cent of GDP	**10.74**	**10.40**	**10.21**	**10.37**	**11.46**	**12.50**	**12.84**

1. Expenditures are in millions of dollars and are reported on a fiscal year basis (1st April to 31 March) except for the child tax credit which is on a calendar year basis.
2. These programmes were replaced by the Child Tax Benefit on 1 January 1993.
3. Prior to 1985-86 this category includes expenditures under the National Institutional and National Industrial Training Programmes. Beginning in 1985-86 this category includes expenditures under the Canadian Jobs Strategy.
4. Federal social assistance and social services for Registered Indians.
5. Includes War Veterans' and Civilian War Allowances and Veterans' and Civilians' Disability Pensions.
Source: Health and Welfare Canada.

Table 17. **Overall social security expenditures**

	1958-59	1980-81	1990-91
Total real expenditures (billions of constant 1993 dollars)	15.6	79.4	127.7
Percentage change		409	61
Real expenditure per capita	913	3 301	4 799
Percentage change		262	45
Real expenditure as a per cent of GDP	**7.8**	**14.7**	**18.3**
Real expenditure as a per cent of total government spending	**32.7**	**38.6**	**41.0**

Source: Based on information in Battle and Torjman (1993). These figures are not cyclically adjusted.

Diagram 20. **THE COST OF LABOUR RELATIVE TO CAPITAL**[1]

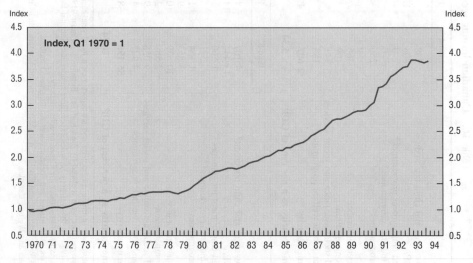

1. Ratio of compensation per employee to machinery and equipment investment deflator.
Source: CANSIM — Statistics Canada; OECD, *Main Economic Indicators*.

Table 18. **Social expenditure in OECD countries**[1]

	Social expenditure share of GDP		Annual growth rate of real GDP (per cent)		Annual growth rate of real social expenditure (per cent)	
	1980	1990	1975-80	1981-90	1975-81	1981-90
Canada	**17.5**	**20.2**	**3.9**	**2.8**	**3.9**	**4.4**
France	24.7	26.7	2.8	2.5	5.2	3.2
Germany	24.6	22.0	2.7	2.5	2.3	1.4
Italy	21.2	26.3	4.0	2.4		4.5
Japan	14.3	14.4	4.4	4.2	6.6	3.9
United Kingdom	18.0	16.9	1.3	3.1		1.8
United States	13.1	12.4	3.0	2.7	1.9	2.0
Average of above countries[2]	19.0	19.9	3.2	2.9		3.0

1. Defined as expenditure on health, education, pensions, unemployment compensation (see Table 19).
2. Unweighted average.
Source: OECD (refer to Table 19).

Table 18 shows real public social spending – defined as expenditure on education, health, pensions and unemployment compensation – trends across the seven largest OECD countries.[34] In 1980, Canada devoted 17.5 per cent of GDP to social programmes compared with an average for major countries of 19 per cent. Subsequently, Canada has experienced significantly stronger real social expenditure growth, highlighting its growing burden both relative to other countries and to GDP.

The development of the share of each major component of social expenditure since the 1970s is shown in Table 19. Most noticeable is the fact that Canada devotes a much larger proportion of government spending to unemployment compensation than do other large OECD countries, while the share going to pensions is lower. It is also the only country to have experienced considerable growth in UI expenditure – as a proportion of government expenditure – in the 1980s.

As can be seen from Table 20, in relation to GDP, Canada spends more on labour-market programmes than the other G7 countries except Germany. This results from spending on income maintenance where Canada is the leader. A relatively small proportion of the substantial expenditure on labour market programmes is allocated to "active" measures, although Canada ranks third in terms of spending on active measures as a per cent of GDP.

Table 19. **Social expenditure programmes in major OECD countries**

Shares of total government expenditure, per cent

	Education share			Health share			Pensions share			Unemployment compensation share		
	1970	1980	1990	1970	1980	1990	1970	1980	1990	1970	1980	1990
Canada	**19.0**	**14.0**	**12.5**	**13.0**	**12.0**	**13.0**	**9.0**	**10.0**	**13.0**	**4.5**	**5.2**	**6.8**
France	13.25[1]	12.3	10.5	12.5[1]	13.1	14.4	21.8	25.0	25.2	0.8	3.5	3.0
Germany	10.6	10.6	8.8	10.5	12.9	12.9	27.0	25.0	23.3	0.8	2.8	2.8
Italy	..	11.4	10.0	..	13.3	12.2	23.2	25.0	27.0	0.5	1.0	0.7
Japan	18.4	16.4	13.4	15.6	15.7	17.3	5.9	14.7	20.4	1.4	1.3	0.8
United Kingdom	12.0[2]	11.6	10.7	9.8[2]	10.6	11.1	11.8	13.5	14.0	1.1	1.9	1.4
United States	14.0	13.4	12.7	2.7	2.8	2.5	16.0	21.0	19.1	1.3	1.8	0.8
Average of above countries[3]	..	12.8	11.2	..	11.5	11.9	16.4	19.0	20.2	1.5	2.5	2.3

1. 1975.
2. 1977.
3. Unweighted average.
Source: OECD, *National Accounts.*

Table 20. **Public expenditure on labour market programmes**

Percentage of GDP, 1991-92

Programme category	**Canada**	France	Germany	Italy	Japan	United Kingdom	United States
1. Employment services and administration	0.22	0.13	0.24	–	0.02	0.15	0.08
2. Labour market training	0.36	0.35	0.59	–	0.03	0.17	0.09
3. Youth measures	0.02	0.23	0.06	–	–	0.18	0.03
4. Subsidised employment	0.02	0.11	0.52	–	0.07	0.03	0.01
5. Measures for the disabled	–	0.06	0.24	–	0.01	0.03	0.05
6. Unemployment compensation	2.25	1.46	1.32	0.60	0.32	1.35	0.59
7. Early retirement for labour market reasons	–	0.47	0.49	0.27	–	–	–
Total	2.87	2.82	3.46	0.88	0.45	1.91	0.84
Total "active measures" (1 to 5)	0.62	0.88	1.64	–	0.13	0.56	0.25
Total income maintenance	2.25	1.94	1.81	0.88	0.32	1.35	0.59

Source: OECD *Employment Outlook*, Paris, OECD, July 1993.

Such a rapid growth in expenditure on social programmes can be attributed
to a number of factors. As noted above, much of the growth was originally due to

the introduction of new programmes and the expansion of coverage and benefits of existing ones. Another important contributing factor is the historically high level of unemployment experienced during the 1980s and early 1990s (Diagram 21). Furthermore, not only did the average unemployment rate rise sharply, the average duration of unemployment and the incidence of long-term unemployment also increased significantly. The number of beneficiaries has also stayed high, despite periods of improved labour market conditions. In addition, until the end of the 1980s, both the labour force participation rate and the fraction of the population employed continued to rise. As a result, programmes such as UI, in which participation is tied to employment, covered an increasing proportion of the population.

Other factors explaining the rise in social expenditure more generally include virtually zero growth in per capita real incomes since the early 1970s, thus removing one of the most effective means of reducing poverty. In addition, both wages and employment income have become more unevenly distributed. As a consequence, a larger proportion of the population has become reliant on transfer income through programmes such as social assistance. Finally, rising poverty and increased reliance on social assistance are also related to changes in family structure – in particular, increased incidence of divorce and in the number of unmarried single parents.

Unemployment insurance disincentives

Changes to the benefit systems in OECD countries appear important when attempting to explain the development of unemployment rates since the 1960s. This is supported by a substantial amount of research on the labour market impacts of UI which has been carried out both in Canada and other OECD countries. This research indicates that benefit entitlements – especially their duration and replacement rates – can increase both the level and duration of unemployment. Furthermore, entitlements to unemployment benefits can partially explain the differences across countries in the structure of unemployment by age, sex and duration. This section briefly summarises the evidence as to the detrimental impact of benefits – especially UI – on employment (a fuller description of the empirical evidence is presented in Annex I) with a view to identifying policy reforms that could improve economic and social outcomes.

Diagram 21. **STRUCTURAL ASPECTS OF UNEMPLOYMENT**

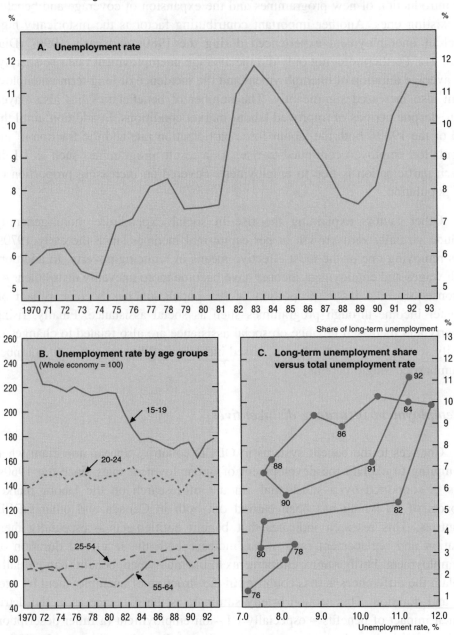

Source: OECD.

Empirical overview

A summary of *cross-country* observations (largely summarised from OECD, 1994, Chapter 7) suggest several adverse effects on work incentives from the provision of benefits such as UI and social assistance. These include:

- those countries with the highest benefit replacement rates generally experience the largest increases in unemployment during recessionary periods;
- growth in unemployment across countries is positively associated with the extent to which benefit replacement rates have increased;
- there are generally positive correlations between the distribution of total unemployment by age, sex, household situation, and duration, and the relative generosity of benefit entitlements of these groups; and
- there is evidence that more effective benefit administration reduces the number of beneficiaries.

UI benefits can have a positive impact on mobility, because they are portable and can be used to finance a shift to areas with better employment prospects. However, an overview of the *time-series* empirical results (see Annex I for a broader discussion) generally supports the cross-country observations made above, albeit to differing degrees. With regard to specific Canadian empirical evidence, the results surveyed indicate a detrimental impact on both job search activities and employment levels, including:

- evidence of higher benefit replacement rates reducing both female job search efforts and the ratio of employed-to-unemployed job search activity;
- evidence that the length of the UI benefit duration influences the duration of unemployment;
- indications that employment terminations (mostly layoffs) cluster around the minimum employment period required to qualify for UI (especially in the Atlantic provinces and in seasonal industries);
- evidence that the layoff/quit ratio responds to the UI qualifying requirements, rising as the requirements have become increasingly stringent with regard to voluntarily leaving employment; and
- a positive relationship between repeat use of UI and seasonal employment opportunities across regions.

Some of the more Canada-specific concerns are elaborated on below, both with regard to labour supply and demand distortions.

Repeat use

UI can lead to a reliance on short employment spells in often marginal industries, supplemented by repeat use of UI. Diagram 22 indicates that UI is becoming increasingly a permanent income support for high-frequency users (those who had eleven or more spells) while it operates as an insurance programme that protects low-frequency users (one to three spells) against labour market risks. Indeed, it appears that in Canada a core of claimants use UI on a regular basis, with an obvious regional pattern dependent on the availability of seasonal work (Diagram 23).[35] This is evident using both hazard functions – the probability of leaving unemployment – and recall expectations – where the employer uses layoffs to moderate output but the employee knows (or expects) a recall is coming. Furthermore, the dynamic effects of UI suggest that current use of the programme is related to past use. Empirical work indicates that the mean

Diagram 22. **PATTERNS OF REPEAT USE OF UNEMPLOYMENT**[1]
Shares of total usage

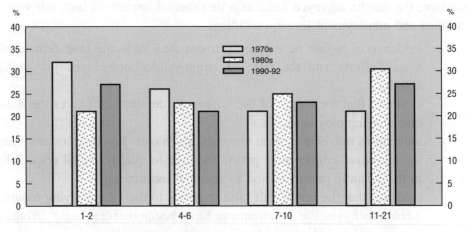

1. Number of spells during 1972-92 period.
Source: Corak M. (1993).

90

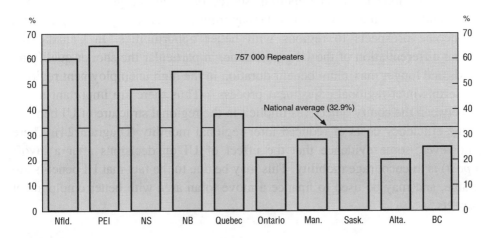

Diagram 23. **UI REPEAT USERS BY PROVINCE**
Percentage of beneficiaries who where repeaters[1] in 1992

1. At least 2 regular claims established in the previous 3 years.
Source: UI Administrative Data, Department of Human Resources Development.

duration of claims rises with repeat use, while the amount of time between claims falls, possibly signalling a gradual deterioration of human capital.

These findings point to a number of significant policy concerns. First it appears that communities within Canada may have adapted to the parameters of the UI system in a way which maximises transfer income in the short run but which creates a long run dependency on marginal employment and transfer income. The fact that repeat use of UI is also prevalent among the young is of particular concern. Young workers, especially those with limited skills and education, have limited income prospects during their early years in the labour force (see Diagram 30). For these individuals, the combination of short employment spells and long periods of UI receipt may appear attractive relative to continuing education or training. This will especially be the case if short-term employment often involves high wages, as is often the case with seasonal work, and therefore greater income while employed and receiving UI benefits.[36]

91

Impediments to labour market mobility

Over the long term, an important source of economic growth and higher living standards is the movement of labour from regions with poor employment and income prospects to regions with better opportunities. In Canada, the regional differentiation of the UI programme, in particular the shorter qualifying periods and longer maximum benefit duration in the high unemployment regions, impede this inter-regional adjustment process.[37] Thus there are important trade-offs between the equity objectives implicit in the regional structure of UI benefits and the efficiency costs of reduced inter-regional mobility (Diagram 24). There is, however, some evidence that the effect of UI on decisions after a layoff (*ex post*) is to encourage mobility. This may be due to the fact that UI benefits are portable, and may be used to finance a move to an area with better employment prospects.

Diagram 24. **NET UI BENEFITS PER CAPITA**[1]

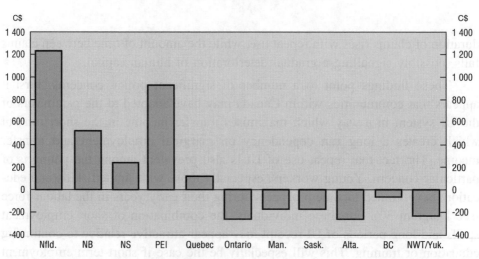

1. 1991 figures. Calculations based on the benefits paid out and the contributions from agents in various regions.
Source: Statistics Canada.

92

Jurisdictional aspects

UI is financed by employer and employee contributions and administered by the Federal government while social assistance programmes are administered by the provinces and are financed on a shared-cost basis by the federal and provincial governments. Provinces therefore have a financial incentive to ensure that individuals who would otherwise be eligible for social assistance receive enough employment to qualify for UI. As a consequence, provinces may introduce "make work" projects to qualify would-be welfare recipients for unemployment insurance. Job creation programmes that may make sense on a cost-benefit basis from a provincial point of view may not be appropriate from a national point of view. Although this is not a unique situation in an OECD context, with several Scandinavian countries experiencing similar distortions, an aspect of this cost-shifting from provincial social assistance to UI warrants policy attention. This is that there is clearly an incentive for provinces to introduce job creation programmes which may not pass a social cost-benefit test. These may be programmes which generate short-term employment for as many participants as possible, rather than programmes which focus on creating longer-term employment for a smaller number of participants or which provide participants with additional education and/or skills.

Subsidising layoffs

Because UI premiums are not experience-rated, the UI programme tends to subsidise firms and industries with unstable employment patterns and tax firms and industries with stable employment patterns. This occurs since employers are able to adjust to shocks in various ways: through inventories, increased efficiency, product diversification, adjusting wages and/or hours worked, and through layoffs and rehires. Given that employers will choose the least cost option, UI benefits bias towards the latter given that workers are less averse to temporary layoffs (*i.e.* firms which rely extensively on layoffs do not have to pay as large a wage premium to attract workers).[38] In Canada this industry cross-subsidisation (Diagram 25) is potentially large (Kesselman, 1983, Chapter 9).

These considerations suggest that, in the absence of experience rating, the UI programme may contribute to employment instability. Recent Canadian empirical analysis supports this view (Corak 1994), highlighting that peaks in the "hazard rate" – the probability that an individual will find employment – occur

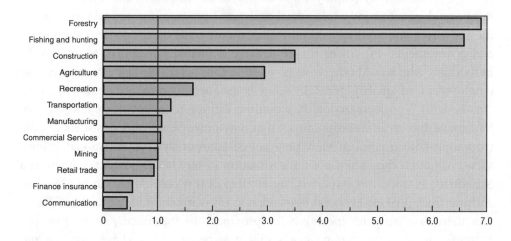

Diagram 25. **BENEFIT-TO-PREMIUM RATIOS FOR SELECTED INDUSTRIES**[1]

1. 1991 figures. Greater than one = beneficiary; less than one = contributor.
Source: Statistics Canada.

just prior to the exhaustion of UI benefits. Furthermore, nearly 50 per cent of the long-term unemployed (more than six months) expect a recall to their former employer. This suggests that employers are actively using the UI programme as a subsidy to their staffing costs. The majority of United States research, much of it utilising the differences that exist across states in the degree to which UI is experience-rated, also indicates that firms respond to the incentives associated with premiums that are only partially experience-rated.[39]

However, careful consideration of some relationships between features of the economic structure and UI costs is important before linking UI benefits to UI premiums. For example, claim rates for small businesses are almost double those of large ones, although industrial sectors vary widely in their reliance on UI (Table 21). Any reform must consider how to minimise the disruption to small business development, as well as address the insurability of rapidly growing non-standard employment (including part-time, short-term and self employment). Together these groups accounted for 45 per cent of all employment growth in the 1980s. These are clearly areas for future research, beyond the scope of this chapter.

Table 21. **Average benefits contribution ratio**

By firm size (1988)		By sector (1990)	
Firm size	Benefits contribution ratio	Sector	Ratio
Less than 5	2.59	Primary	4.93
5 to 10	1.58	Mining	0.92
10 to 20	1.36	Manufacturing	1.17
20 to 50	1.16	Construction	3.38
50 to 100	1.01	Transportation	1.28
100 to 200	0.89	Commerce	0.44
200 to 500	0.70	Wholesale trade	0.84
500 to 1 000	0.58	Retail trade	0.81
1 000 to 1 500	0.52	Finance	0.63
1 500 to 2 500	0.39	Business services	0.98
More than 5 000	0.44	Government	0.51
		Education	0.40
		Health	0.45
		Food and beverage services	1.67
		Other	1.39
Total	1.00	Total	1.00

Source: Human Resources Development, Canada

Implications of high and rising payroll taxes

The rise in Canadian payroll taxes (which include UI premiums) has led to a growing concern that they dampen employment prospects.[40] Indeed, the changes to the UI programme introduced in the February 1994 Budget had as an objective the stabilisation of UI premiums despite the UI account being in substantial deficit.[41] However, the UI programme is not the only source of rising payroll taxes. The Canada and Quebec Pension Plans are also financed by employer and employee contributions, both of which have risen sharply in recent years.[42] This is equally the case of the costs of workers' compensation programmes, which vary across provinces and are financed by payroll taxes (Diagram 26). In addition, four provinces have introduced payroll taxes for general revenue purposes (Quebec 1970, Manitoba 1982, Ontario 1990, and Newfoundland 1990). In three of these provinces the revenue from payroll taxes exceeds that from the corporate income tax.[43] The timing of UI payroll tax changes is also of particular concern. As Table 12 indicates, UI premiums fell in the expansionary period 1985-89 but rose sharply during the recession of 1990-91 and at the beginning of the subse-

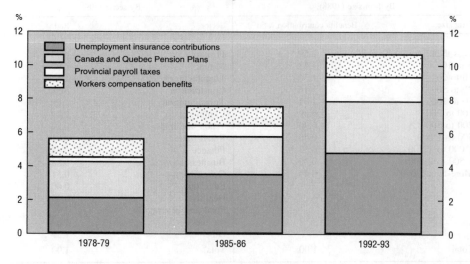

Diagram 26. **USE OF PAYROLL TAXES**

Per cent of wages and salaries

Legend:
- Unemployment insurance contributions
- Canada and Quebec Pension Plans
- Provincial payroll taxes
- Workers compensation benefits

1978-79   1985-86   1992-93

Source: Department of Finance, Canada.

quent recovery when employment growth was weak. Part of this increase reflects a major policy change which shifted the full costs of the UI programme to employers and employees. Hence, apart from issues about increases in UI-related payroll taxes, the pro-cyclical nature of premium adjustments also requires careful assessment, given its potential to exacerbate the cyclical fluctuations in employment and unemployment.

The concern regarding rising payroll taxes (such as employers' UI contributions) is related to the fact that they raise the cost of employing labour over and above the wage paid. Furthermore, income taxes, employees' social security contributions and consumption taxes all reduce the financial returns to supplying labour. In sum, all of these taxes are important in determining employment levels since they directly influence the rate of return from decisions to enter the labour market and increase hours worked, to undertake training, and to bargain for a higher gross wage. Although the net effect of a rise in taxes – which operates through both labour supply and demand decisions – are theoretically ambiguous,[44] in practice they generally result in a lower level of employment.

96

The magnitude of the subsequent decline in employment depends positively on the degree of wage rigidity in the economy.

The net effect of tax changes on employment can be summarised using the overall "tax wedge", that is, the difference between the cost of employing someone and the consumption which can eventually be financed from supplying this work.[45] As an illustration, Table 22 provides tax wedge estimates for a number of OECD countries. These can be interpreted as the difference between the cost to an employer of increasing labour incomes by one unit and the average value of consumption which a worker can obtain out of that increase in the gross

Table 22.   **Overall marginal tax wedges in a number of OECD countries**

	1978	1981	1985	1989	1991/92
Australia	38.4	37.4	51.6	45.0	43.2
Belgium	58.3	62.1	64.9	65.6	65.4
Canada	**39.2**	**40.0**	**42.7**	**40.9**	**54.4**
Denmark	66.4	68.8	71.9	68.6	68.6
Finland	62.3	61.6	62.6	65.9	63.4
France	55.0	57.8	60.8	61.6	62.0
Germany	66.2	63.4	66.8	65.5	62.5
Italy	49.6	55.7	62.0	58.7	59.5
Japan	26.4	21.2	22.6	21.5	21.9
Netherlands	61.1	69.0	71.5	68.0	69.8
Norway	66.3	68.0	71.2	70.0	58.2
Spain	44.0	44.9	52.2	52.3	52.5
Sweden	74.4	74.2	69.4	68.6	60.0
United Kingdom	50.9	50.8	53.1	48.5	48.9
United States	44.2	50.2	48.0	38.1	38.4
Overall average	53.5	55.0	58.1	55.9	55.3
OECD Europe	59.5	61.5	64.2	63.0	61.0
European Community	56.4	59.0	62.9	61.1	61.2
OECD non-Europe	37.0	37.2	41.2	36.4	39.5

Note: The overall tax wedge includes employees' and employers' social security contributions, personal income taxes and consumption taxes. Social security contributions and income taxes are calculated by applying the tax rules to the level of earnings of an Average Production Worker (APW) based on the OECD annual publication (*The Tax and Benefit Position of Production Workers*). Consumption tax rates are calculated from aggregate tax and national income data. Social security contributions include only those paid to the public sector; contributions to the private sector are ignored despite their importance in some countries (*e.g.* Finland). Social security contributions in some countries are closely linked to expected benefits, therefore treating them in the aggregate as if they are simply taxes is a simplification. Payroll taxes which are not earmarked for social security are not taken into account in these calculations. No account is taken of "non-standard" reliefs, such as those for mortgage payments (see *The Tax and Benefit Position of Production Workers* for a detailed discussion of limitations). Furthermore, the tax wedges in this table only concern one point on the earnings distribution (the APW case), and someone on this income level may have consumption patterns which lead to different consumption tax payments from those derived from aggregate data.
Source: OECD (1994a).

wage (see OECD, 1994, Chapter 8). With regard to Canada, the tax wedge has gone from being significantly below the OECD average in 1978 to around the average more recently. Canada has also experienced the largest increase of all countries displayed, with the wedge now significantly above other non-European OECD countries. In addition, there has been a significant rise in the tax wedge between 1989 and 1992, reflecting in part the increase in UI premiums as the system shifted to a fully-financed basis. In sum, over one-half of the increase since the late 1970s in employers' wage costs reflects higher taxes, compared to one-fifth in Japan and one-third in the United States.

Using these data, cross-country empirical results (summarised in Annex I) highlight the detrimental effect that rising payroll taxes can have on employment levels, especially in rigid wage economies. The results indicate a weak positive correlation between the size of a country's tax wedge and the unemployment rate. This is supported by country specific time-series evidence, indicating that a tax increase will raise labour costs – although there is less agreement on the extent of this effect and its consequences for employment, on the speed with which any effect takes place, and on whether the effects are the same across different tax types.

With regard to Canada, Coe (1990) concludes that employers' payroll taxes increased the natural rate of unemployment by 1.5 percentage points in the 1970s, and by another percentage point subsequently. On the other hand, personal income taxes and indirect taxes were not found to be significant. This is supported by evidence (OECD, 1994, Chapter 8), summarised in Annex I, which shows that Canada has relatively rigid wages in the face of a rise in marginal tax rates, with labour costs adjusting by the full amount of a marginal tax increase, leading to an eventual decline in employment.[46] This explains, in part, why the United States unemployment rate has been consistently lower than Canada's since the 1980s, especially in an environment where wage flexibility has become increasingly important as a means of regaining employment (Diagram 27).

Summary

Canada's UI programme appears to create labour market distortions that can lead directly to inefficiency as well as increased unemployment. The accepted channel for this is the programmes' generosity and its effect on incentives to both demand and supply labour. The evidence discussed above suggests that UI bene-

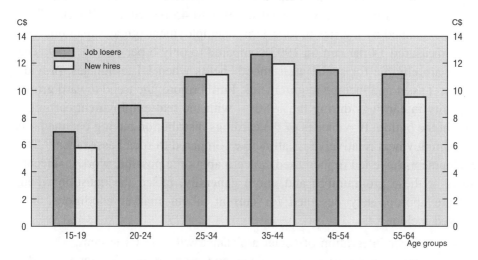

Diagram 27. **WAGES PAID TO JOB LOSERS AGAINST NEW HIRES**

1988 data, dollars per hour

Source: Labour Market Activity Survey.

fits encourage marginal attachment to the labour force by promoting unstable and seasonal industries through the subsidisation of temporary layoffs. In sum, the net effect of the provision of UI benefits may imply a reverse situation where benefit provision leads to unemployment. These concerns are pressing in Canada, where unemployment has increasingly tended to persist, even in times of economic expansion, and transfer dependency has become an increasingly important phenomenon.

Social assistance concerns

In addition to the distortions created by the UI system, both the dramatic rise in welfare spending since the early 1980s and the associated labour-market disincentive effects constitute a serious challenge for the federal and provincial governments. As noted above, the design of social assistance was originally that the federal government operate a national unemployment insurance programme for employables, and the provinces provide income support to those unable to work due to illness, disability or family responsibilities. In this light, the provincial social assistance programmes have paid little attention to work incentives, despite the proportion of the social assistance caseload regarded as employable rising substantially (from 36 per cent in 1981 to 45 per cent in 1992).[47] This is largely explained by the rise in long-term unemployment (greater than one-year), which measured 14 per cent in 1993 compared to only 6 per cent in 1989. These people are eligible for social assistance benefits when UI terminates, providing they meet asset and income requirements. Furthermore, the trend toward growing inequality in earnings during the 1980s – with the real employment earnings of those in the bottom two deciles of the earnings distribution having declined – has made employment relatively less attractive compared to social assistance.[48] These developments have led to increased concern about the possible work disincentive effects of these programmes and, more generally, raised the question whether they are appropriately designed for current labour market conditions. Issues involved include:

- – a better integration of social assistance with the UI system;
- – a better integration with policies and programmes designed to aid the transition from school to work; and
- – more focus on mechanisms to improve the employability and potential earnings of social assistance recipients.

These issues are discussed below, following an examination of the specific concerns associated with the current social assistance.

Welfare traps

Many social assistance programmes operate under the basic principle that income support is withdrawn if one or more family members enter the labour market and earn an income (provided the non-exempted income exceeds the household's needs, as quantified in provincial and social assistance legislation). This leads to "welfare traps" whereby the implicit marginal tax rate facing employment is very high, usually due to the interaction of the tax system and the withdrawal of social assistance benefits.[49] These implicit marginal tax rates can often imply that individuals receive no – or very little – extra income for their effort in the labour market, thereby reducing any work incentive.

Such welfare traps are prevalent in the Canadian social assistance schemes. High marginal tax rates exist, despite all provinces having some form of an earnings exemption – under which there is no reduction in welfare support for small amounts of employment income – and some provinces not reducing welfare support on a strict dollar-for-dollar basis in response to employment income. In addition to any possible reduction in welfare payments for those taking up employment, the removal of provisions such as subsidised housing, dental care, and child care assistance also significantly raises the implicit marginal tax rates, often to over 100 per cent. Finally, the tax and transfer system for labour force participants (federal and provincial income taxes, and payroll taxes) all act to reduce the after-tax income associated with gaining employment, further reducing work incentives. The consequence of these provisions, which vary according to province and by family size and composition within provinces, is a complex set of implicit marginal tax rates facing welfare recipients who may wish to enter or re-enter the labour market. Illustrative examples of implicit tax rates are provided for Ontario and Quebec in Fortin (1985), for British Columbia and New Brunswick in Kesselman and Riddell (1991), and for Ontario in Battle and Torjman (1993c). Diagram 28 illustrates the level of social assistance income in Ontario, the most populous province.

Diagram 28. **ONTARIO SOCIAL ASSISTANCE INCOME**
Equivalents for various demographics groups (C$)

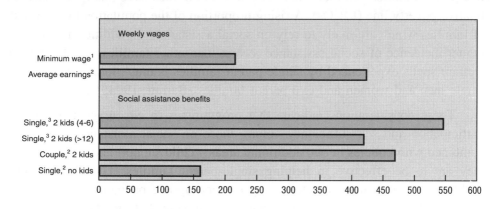

1. Based on minimum wage of C$ 5.40/hour.
2. Average weekly earnings for hourly paid workers, including overtime.
3. Monthly rent is C$ 385 for single, C$ 715 for couple with kids.
Source : Statistics Canada.

In addition to these static effects, concern has been expressed about possible dynamic effects associated with receiving social assistance. For example, there may be "duration dependence" in the sense that the likelihood of leaving welfare may decline the longer one spends on social assistance. Alternatively, for those experiencing multiple welfare spells, there may be "incidence dependence" in the sense that the probability of leaving welfare may decline with each successive social assistance spell. These effects may occur because participants' human capital, and thus potential earnings, may deteriorate during welfare spells or because there may be reduced stigma the longer one spends on welfare or the more frequently welfare spells are experienced. Little is known about the magnitude of these dynamic effects in Canada, although a recent study (Barrett, 1994) finds evidence of duration dependence in social assistance spells in British Columbia.

Changing family structures

Demographic factors have also played a significant role in the rise of social expenditures in the last decade. The proportion of one-parent families with children has been rising, increasing from 10.7 to 16.4 per cent of all families with children between 1980 and 1992. Furthermore, the proportion of single mothers working has declined (Diagram 29). Women now head more than 80 per cent of one-parent families and more than half of such families have incomes below the relative poverty line (LICOs). A rising proportion of the population thus consists of families which are likely to rely on social assistance. In addition to having a higher incidence of social assistance receipt than other families, the duration of welfare spells experienced by single-parent families is much longer than that of single men and women and two parent families (Barrett, 1994; Cragg, 1994).

These considerations indicate that programmes to encourage labour-force participation and self-sufficiency among those on social assistance need to be combined with policies in two additional areas – child support and child care – if they are to be effective in helping single-parent families. The child support problem is in part that of determining the appropriate payment (usually to be made by the father) to ensure that both parents contribute to the child's well-being. However, the larger challenge is the monitoring and enforcement of these contributions. Although public enforcement of child support payments has increased in Canada and there have been improvements in mechanisms for

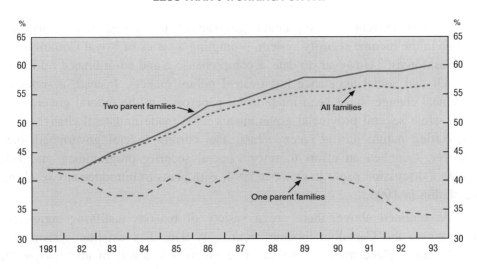

Diagram 29. **PERCENTAGE OF MOTHERS WITH CHILDREN LESS THAN 6 WORKING FOR PAY**

Source: Department of Human Resources Development, Canada (1994*b*).

handling inter-jurisdictional (usually inter-provincial) claims, further policy attention in this respect is warranted.

Growing dependency ratios

Canadian social assistance programmes act as income support of last resort, both for those unable to work and for those who wish to work but cannot obtain employment and do not have other means of support. Increases in welfare spending and in the number of recipients during economic downturns are therefore expected to occur. However, the fact that real welfare expenditures and the number of social assistance recipients declined only modestly during the 1985-89 period and remained substantially above their pre-recession levels is a serious concern. The related upward trend in the proportion of the population receiving social assistance since the introduction of CAP is also worrying. These developments have received the attention of federal and provincial policy-makers; however, as discussed below, more fundamental changes will probably be required if these trends are to be arrested or reversed.

Reforming the system

Both the current and the previous government have recognised the need for change in the income security system, prompting a series of Royal Commissions and Taskforces.[50] However, to date, a comprehensive and co-ordinated reform of both UI and social assistance has evaded policy makers. Instead, a series of piecemeal changes have been made to UI generosity at the federal government level, while several provincial governments have made unilateral changes of a cost-cutting nature during recent years. The current federal government has, however, launched an effort to reform social security programmes, and will release a discussion paper in October 1994, with plans to introduce any resulting legislation in 1995.

As outlined above, there are a variety of reasons justifying significant revisions to the Canadian income security system. The existing system was largely put in place during a period of relatively low levels of unemployment, little long-term unemployment, reasonably good income and employment prospects[51] and relatively long-term employment attachments. In this environment, unemployment insurance was intended to provide income support for those experiencing temporary and, on average, brief spells of unemployment while welfare payments were intended to provide a basic level of income to those unable to work. The labour market of the 1990s is, however, vastly different. The average level of unemployment has risen during each of the past four decades, while there has also been an increase in the number of long-term unemployed.[52] In particular, although the size of the youth cohort entering the labour market has been significantly smaller since the beginning of the 1980s,[53] the labour market situation facing youths has deteriorated more recently (Betcherman and Morissette, 1993) – especially for those with limited education (Diagram 30). The 1980s and early 1990s have also been characterised by much more lasting job loss than took place in earlier decades. In these circumstances, there may be a greater need for training, re-training and mobility assistance and less emphasis on passive income support.

Adjusting the Unemployment Insurance programme

UI reform has frequently been debated in the past decade. Although there have been a series of amendments to the UI Act (most recently in 1990, 1993 and

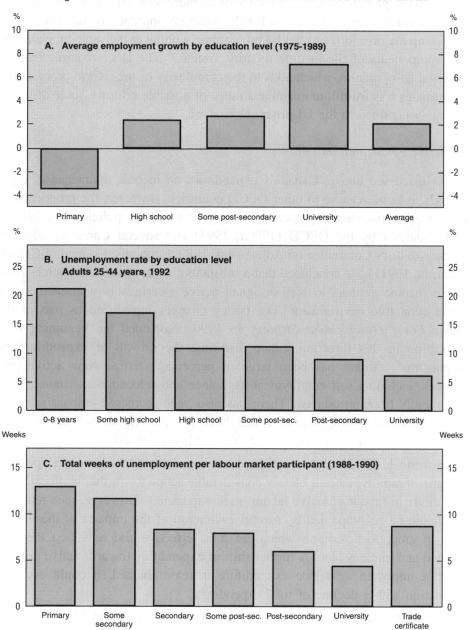

Diagram 30. **EMPLOYMENT AND UNEMPLOYMENT BY EDUCATION LEVEL**

A. Average employment growth by education level (1975-1989)

Primary High school Some post-secondary University Average

B. Unemployment rate by education level
Adults 25-44 years, 1992

0-8 years Some high school High school Some post-sec. Post-secondary University

C. Total weeks of unemployment per labour market participant (1988-1990)

Primary Some secondary Secondary Some post-sec. Post-secondary University Trade certificate

Source: Labour Market Activity Survey, Canada.

1994), reform proposals have generally been more sweeping than the changes ultimately made. Part of the reason for this cautious approach is the difficulty of introducing major reforms to the UI programme without at the same time altering other components of the income security system.[54] The latter requires federal-provincial co-operation, which adds to the complexity of the reform process. For these reasons it is fruitful to examine a range of possible reforms, some of which are largely confined to the UI programme alone.

Active labour market policies

As discussed above, Canada's expenditure on income maintenance, especially UI, is large relative to other OECD countries. However, the proportion of labour market programme expenditure devoted to active policies is relatively small. Analysis by the OECD (1990a, 1993) and several Canadian advisory bodies (Advisory Committee on Adjustment, 1989; Economic Council of Canada of Canada, 1991) have concluded that a substantial reallocation of resources from passive income support to well-designed active measures is warranted in the current economic environment. The policy changes introduced as part of the *Labour Force Development Strategy* in 1990 constituted the beginning of a reallocation in this direction. Since that time the growth of expenditure on UI-sponsored training has been large in percentage terms. New active programmes, including self-employment assistance and relocation assistance, have subsequently been introduced. There has also been increased emphasis on job search assistance – programmes which have proven very cost-effective in UI experiments carried out in the United States (Meyer, 1992).

Nevertheless, although UI expenditures on active labour market policies have grown rapidly, there is clearly considerable scope for further reallocation of expenditure in favour of active labour market measures. However, such reallocation should be accompanied by careful evaluation of the impacts of these measures, in order to determine which are most effective and how best they are designed and implemented. A further shift of expenditure towards active policies does not imply an aggregate expenditure increase. Indeed, it could occur in conjunction with a decline of total expenditure.

An important feature of the Labour Force Development Strategy is the greater involvement of the private sector in UI-sponsored training and other developmental uses of the UI fund. This change continues the process initiated with the *Canadian Jobs Strategy* (CJS) in 1985 which provided for greater private sector involvement in government-funded training programmes, increased emphasis on on-the-job training and work experience, and reduced use of class-room training. Evaluations of the various CJS programmes generally conclude that this shift in focus improved their impacts on trainees (Employment and Immigration Canada, 1992).

A recent evaluation of UI-sponsored training provides additional evidence on the consequences of this approach (Human Resources Development Canada, 1993). The study examined the impacts on trainees in three CJS programmes (Job Development, Job Entry and Skill Shortages) as well as participants in the Feepayer option (claimants who receive UI but are exempted from having to search for a job while taking training, although they or a third party must pay for the cost of the training) and UI claimants who take part-time training without needing the approval of the UI authorities. The comparison group consisted of a group of regular UI claimants. The estimated impacts varied by programme and by cohort. Large positive impacts on earnings were found for the 1988 cohort in the Feepayer, Job Entry and Skill Shortages programmes. However, for the 1989 cohort, which completed training after the onset of the 1990-92 recession, positive and significant impacts on earnings were found only for the Job Entry programme. The results of this evaluation study, which are only very briefly summarised here, are moderately encouraging for the further expansion of train-ing programmes for those who could otherwise receive UI benefits alone.

Standardising entrance requirements and benefit durations

The regional differentiation of the UI programme – especially the features introduced in the late 1970s – appears to be effective in transferring income into high unemployment regions from other parts of the country. However, this feature of the current programme has numerous undesirable consequences, as discussed above. On the basis of these considerations, both the *Royal Commission on the Economic Union and Development Prospects for Canada* (1985) and the *Commission of Inquiry on Unemployment Insurance* (1986) – the Forget Commission – recommended that regional differentiation of the programme be ended. The more recent empirical studies reviewed earlier only serve to reinforce the view that the undesirable consequences of the regional differences in qualify-ing periods and maximum benefit duration are significant.

While the 1990 reforms increased the degree of regional differentiation (qualification periods were increased and maximum benefit durations reduced in low unemployment regions, but were not significantly altered in high unemployment regions), the reforms introduced in the February 1994 Budget moved in the opposite direction. The case for continuing this process appears strong, even if gradual change may be the preferred route given the extent to which individuals, employers and even governments appear to have adapted to the incentives created by the current arrangements. The 1994 reforms also strengthen the link between maximum benefit duration and prior work experience,[55] with increased benefit durations for those with long prior employment spells and reduced benefit durations for those with short prior employment ones. A co-ordinated approach to further change in these directions (reducing the regional differentiation of the programme and strengthening the link between work experience and benefit entitlement) would be desirable.

Experience-rating insurance premiums

The advantages of experience-rating of employer premiums are evident from the previous discussion above. In particular, such a premium structure provides to employers the incentives to economise on unemployment generated by layoffs when alternative adjustment mechanisms would be preferable from an employment point of view. Experience rating would also reduce the need for a special programme to encourage worksharing. The current worksharing programme, which is funded under the "developmental uses" provisions of the UI Act, is based on the fact that employers and employees may prefer to respond to reductions in demand by laying off, rather than reducing hours of work for the entire workforce. This preference for layoffs arises because the UI programme is structured to provide benefits to those unemployed but not to those faced with reduced hours of work. The unintended bias can be eliminated by changing either UI financing or benefit provisions. Although a primary objection to experience-rated premiums is the additional administrative complexity, given that the UI programme is nation-wide and has good administrative data, some variation in UI premiums according to the extent to which the employer generates layoffs could be introduced at modest cost. Further examination of the costs and benefits of experience-rated premiums would thus appear worthwhile.

The implementation of the new benefit schedule described above addresses many incentive issues, especially those related to employees. By making it less attractive for workers to qualify for, and maintain, UI benefits, they will be less likely to remain with employers who are offering only limited periods of work. This would have a similar effect to the experience rating for employer premiums and would certainly prove easier to administer, since UI deals with individuals rather than employers.

Reforming the wider social safety net

Although reforming the UI programme is itself a major challenge, it is only one component – albeit a large and important one – of the income security system. Proposals to reform UI need to be assessed in the context of their implications for the entire income security system. In this regard, policies to encourage social assistance recipients to enter or re-enter the labour force have received considerable attention in Canada during the past decade. This shift from primarily passive income support to active policies to promote employment is a consequence of the developments discussed in the previous section: substantial increases in welfare spending, increases in the proportion of recipients classified as employable, and the large proportion of the welfare caseload made up of two-parent families and single men and women without families.

Concern about these developments led to the 1985 "Four Corners Agreement" signed by the Federal Departments of Health and Welfare (which at that time administered the Canada Assistance Plan) and Employment and Immigration Canada (which administered employment and training programmes under the Canadian Jobs Strategy) and their provincial counterparts (provincial ministries of social assistance and employment, training and skills upgrading). Subsequently a large number of initiatives designed to enhance the skills of welfare recipients and encourage employment have been undertaken. Careful evaluation of these initiatives will be essential in determining which programmes are effective and how best they are administered. Some evaluations have been completed and others are under way. At the federal level, the recent merging of the welfare component of the former Department of Health and Welfare with the department which administers the UI and employment and training programmes – producing the combined Department of Human Resources Development – is a positive step towards better co-ordination of policies. However, significant improvements in this respect are also clearly dependent on federal-provincial co-operation.

Integration versus income support

Many of the initiatives launched since the "Four Corners Agreement" involve one or more of the following for welfare recipients: wage subsidies to provide on-the-job training and work experience; job search assistance; educational, vocational and technical classroom training offered in community colleges and institutes; and public sector employment programmes to provide work experience. Evaluations of these programmes indicate that they can be successful, albeit to varying degrees. For example, employability initiatives for social assistance recipients under the Canadian Jobs Strategy have been evaluated using quasi-experimental methods which compare the post-programme behaviour of participants and a comparison group of non-participants (Employment and Immigration Canada, 1993). It was found that both earnings and employability increased substantially as a result of the programme, although post-programme dependence on UI increased as a result of more individuals becoming "employable", and thus being eligible for UI benefits if employment ceased.

Evaluations of programmes carried out in British Columbia (Ministry of Social Services, Province of British Columbia, 1992) have the added advantage of following participants for an extended period of time (over five years) after the cessation of a particular programme. The results indicate that:

- *on-the-job training with wage subsidies* tended to improve employment of former welfare recipients while social assistance dependency declined, although this was offset partially by increased UI dependence;
- *on-the-job training via public employment* programmes reduced welfare dependence in the short run but had little long term impact, while UI dependency increased substantially;
- the impact of *classroom training* was found to be dependent on the type of training. Career, Technical and Vocational courses had the largest positive impact, Academic courses had a modest impact and Adult Basic Education had little, if any, impact;
- finally, *job search assistance* programmes (which are much less expensive than training and wage subsidies) were found to reduce welfare dependence, primarily by helping recipients to obtain employment more quickly than they would otherwise have done.

In general, these findings are consistent with United States evidence which also indicates a substantial positive return to these types of programmes (Meyer, 1992).

These evaluations, and those of subsequent initiatives, are important in setting priorities for programme funding and in improving the way programmes are administered. The fact that some programmes appear to be effective implies that participants leave welfare even more quickly than they would otherwise have done. However, an important evaluation issue which has not yet been adequately assessed is the permanence of these effects and the costs of these programmes. Given the substantial amount of repeat use of social assistance, this aspect would require attention.

Supporting the working poor

The high implicit marginal tax rates facing welfare recipients on employment income is a serious obstacle to their labour force participation. However, the central dilemma to reducing the "welfare trap" – essentially by lowering the benefit reduction rate – is that it often implies that some people who were previously not entitled to a benefit become eligible, thereby raising their effective marginal tax rates.[56] Thus, the additional advantage of lowering one individual's effective tax rate against raising someone else's must be carefully assessed. Furthermore, although an overall cut in taxes on labour, with no compensating tax increases, would unambiguously improve employment prospects, budget considerations often do not allow this. Instead, increases in other taxes are necessary, potentially further reducing labour supply and the incentive to increase skill levels. Generally speaking, employment effects of shifting a given overall tax burden will likely be modest. Nevertheless, three facts remain significant: certain groups are more responsive to tax changes than others;[57] the responsiveness to tax changes declines the greater the number of hours already worked; and tax changes can promote both entry and exit from the labour market. As a result, most policy discussion tends to be focused on shifting the tax burden away from labour (especially the relatively low-paid), possibly moving them to other wider-based tax sources (as discussed in OECD, 1994).

Another solution to the welfare trap dilemma is to provide a temporary earnings subsidy to welfare recipients to enter work. Such a subsidy could be effective in promoting self-sufficiency if beneficiaries' employment income exceeds their welfare earnings when the subsidy expires. Earnings growth could occur because of wage rises associated with accumulated work experience, increased hours of work, or switching to better paying jobs. This policy is being tested in a major experiment funded by the federal Human Resources Development Department in the provinces of New Brunswick and British Columbia. The "Self-Sufficiency Project" employs an experiment design in which single parents on welfare are selected randomly and asked to participate. Those who agree to do so (*i.e.* the vast majority) are assigned at random to one of two groups: a treatment group (*i.e.* those who are eligible to receive the supplement if they leave welfare and provide proof of full-time work) and a control group (*i.e.* those who remain on welfare and are not eligible for the supplement). An essential feature of the experiment is a work requirement which stipulates that only full-time jobs (*i.e.* jobs with a minimum of 30 hours of work per week) are to be considered. Credible evidence about the effects of this policy should be forthcoming. The major concern about the policy being tested is that the required degree of earnings growth may not materialise. For single parent families on welfare (the specific group being enrolled in the Project), the employment income necessary to exceed social assistance income is substantial, well above the minimum wage in both New Brunswick and British Columbia.

An alternative approach to the welfare trap problem is income supplementation for the working poor, as recommended by a number of Canadian advisory bodies.[58] This has been advocated both to provide improved incentives for labour force participation and to reduce poverty, especially with regard to families with children who face the steepest marginal tax rates. However, when considering reforms to ease the welfare trap of working parents, it is important to separate the goals of day care provision – which is usually dependent on labour force attachment – and child income support – which is aimed at reducing child poverty. The provision of the former will not necessarily resolve all welfare trap concerns, given that high marginal tax rates on employment income remain, although it will become increasingly necessary as other incentives to join the labour force grow.

With regard to reducing child poverty, at present the federal Child Tax Benefit includes an "earned-income supplement" payable to families with one or more children and low employment earnings.[59] This eases the transition from welfare to work since the income support is independent of whether the family is currently receiving welfare payments. Increases in the earned-income supplement would be one way to improve work incentives and reduce poverty among the working poor. In this regard, proposals made in Ontario's (1994) "Turning Point" document appear promising. The introduction of a Child Income programme is suggested – amongst other reforms – which provides an income-tested guaranteed annual income for children. This also represents a possible avenue for more integration with federal welfare provision. Nevertheless, Ontario has recently decided not to pursue this proposal, citing that it was too expensive.

Quebec's approach to social assistance reform – the Parental Wage Assistance (PWA) programme (implemented in 1988) – is also instructive. This contains three components: a supplement to employment income, reimbursement of approximately 55 per cent of eligible day care expenses, and a housing allowance. Importantly, since Quebec has its own personal income tax, the PWA system is also well integrated with the structure of federal social assistance benefits.[60] In particular, a guiding principle is that welfare benefits should not exceed the financial resources of other low income groups, or of workers paid at the minimum wage. The net result of the programme is that workers with modest incomes and dependent children are encouraged to remain in the workforce. Moreover, UI and welfare recipients will have an incentive to join the workforce. The Quebec system incorporates the desirable feature of a lower marginal implicit tax rate on employment. However, the system is extremely complicated to administer and has undergone several changes since its introduction. Furthermore, dependency remains high, making it difficult to gauge its success.

In sum, a number of instructive projects are occurring among provincial governments in Canada, indicating a general willingness to improve on the current social assistance delivery system. They all involve to differing degrees either increased work and training requirements to qualify for benefit receipt and/or aspects of a negative income tax to encourage work incentives for low income groups. Although most projects are in their infancy with long-term results unavailable, care should be taken in the design of both federal and provincial programmes to ensure that they are integrated, thereby avoiding unnecessarily high effective tax rates for higher income groups as well as further incentive distortions. Furthermore, these programmes often imply increased expenditure, hence a detailed cost-benefit analysis of these efforts is necessary to make an informed judgement as to their usefulness.

Concluding remarks

Canada's income security system consists of a complex set of programmes which have evolved over several decades. Particularly important changes to the system were made in the 1960s and early 1970s. During the subsequent period expenditures on income security have risen dramatically in real terms. The current level of expenditure on these programmes is now a serious challenge facing governments and taxpayers. This chapter has largely focused on unemployment insurance and social assistance, the two programmes which provide a "safety net" for the bulk of the population. Both programmes have extensive coverage: UI covers about 90 per cent of the labour force and welfare is available to any individual or family in situations of established financial need. The importance of these two programmes has become evident during the 1980s and 1990s when many Canadians were adversely affected by two major recessions and dislocation due to economic restructuring. However, the current trend of expenditure on UI and social assistance probably cannot be sustained in the current fiscal environment. Furthermore, these programmes are no longer appropriately designed for current economic and labour market conditions. Indeed, they contain disincentives to work, which may contribute to a growing dependency on transfer income.

This points to the necessity of a number of reforms which could improve the operation of the system:

- greater use of active labour market programmes involving training, retraining, job search assistance, relocation assistance and self-employment assistance. Canadian policy has already been moving in this direction, but further reallocation within the existing UI expenditure envelope may be warranted following careful evaluation of the current programmes;
- less regional differentiation of the programme in the form of qualifying requirements and maximum benefit durations and increased linkage between previous work experience and maximum benefit durations. The recent UI reforms introduced in the February 1994 Budget are appropriate in this respect, but further changes along these lines also appear warranted;

- experience rating of employer UI premiums. This change on the financing side of UI would provide employers with the incentive to economise on unemployment, when it is cost effective to do so, thus leading to reduced layoffs and employment instability. Experience rating would also remove the need for special programmes to promote worksharing;
- more effective benefit administration (especially in the sense of improving incentive structures for work creation), especially given the fact that the number of UI beneficiaries has failed to decline with unemployment. This is a necessary condition for creating an overall labour market which balances a reasonable degree of income protection without damping job search incentives and the ability to offer jobs and provide adequate job search assistance.

The above assessment of social assistance also points to reforms which could improve performance. In most Canadian jurisdictions there has been increased emphasis on programmes to enhance employability and assist welfare recipients to return to work. Further movement in this direction appears warranted given the characteristics of the current welfare caseload. Evaluations of several of these initiatives are encouraging for their continued use and expansion. In addition to these programmes, more attention should be paid to the fact that most welfare recipients face very high implicit marginal tax rates on employment income. These could be reduced and the income of the working poor supplemented in order that families on welfare are financially better off in the labour force. Although a variety of options exist for bringing about such changes, any revenue neutral tax change introduced to this effect should involve a shift to the broadest possible tax alternatives.

Again it is important to reiterate that these are some of the directions that reform may take. As noted, the changes being considered encompass a much broader set of programmes and issues than those discussed in this chapter. These could take the form of:
- incremental programme-by-programme reforms, similar to the recent changes to unemployment insurance;
- more fundamental changes to the structure of programmes. For example, it is possible to consider an unemployment-insurance system that would distinguish between workers with a reasonably stable attachment to the

labour force and others who use UI repeatedly. While the former would benefit from traditional earnings-replacement insurance, an employability-oriented approach could be introduced for the latter;
– reallocations and rationalisation across existing programming boundaries. This would involve changing the mix of social assistance and tax benefits like the child tax credit, or the mix of income security and social services such as employability services.

The directions for reform suggested in this chapter would make sense regardless of which of the above options is chosen.

IV. Conclusions

Canada's economic performance has improved during the past twelve months or so. After an extended period of sluggish growth, the recovery has gathered momentum, with real GDP expanding at an annual rate of 4¹/₂ per cent in the first half of 1994. At the same time, the upturn has become more broadly based, as household spending and non-residential construction are increasingly supplementing exports and business investment in machinery and equipment as a source of demand. Meanwhile, despite a significant depreciation of the Canadian dollar, inflation has remained subdued (at 1¹/₂ per cent adjusted for cuts in tobacco taxes). Nonetheless, large imbalances persist in some areas. Unemployment – albeit declining – still exceeds 10 per cent. The current-account deficit remains around 4 per cent of GDP, as strong investment in machinery and equipment is boosting imports. Moreover, the public-sector deficit remains excessive.

Disinflation along with strong business investment has provided an environment conducive to sustained non-inflationary growth and a gradual unwinding of economic imbalances. Indeed, with output growth projected to average 4 per cent in 1994 and 1995, the ongoing recovery is expected to be strong enough to bring about significant declines in unemployment and the budget deficit. In addition, the substantial improvement in Canada's competitive position – due to both exchange-rate depreciation and continued low inflation – should allow continued rapid growth in exports and a progressive narrowing of the current-account deficit.

There are some risks attached to this favourable outlook, however. The gains in competitiveness might not suffice to compensate for Canada's high import propensity, or to offset the adverse effect on exports of a possible slowdown of activity in the United States; this could lead to slower economic growth and a persistent large external deficit. Moreover, weaker activity or higher interest rates than projected could result in an increased government deficit. Financial-market concerns about slow progress in eliminating these twin deficits, in addition to those about the future of the federation, may limit the scope for a narrowing of Canada/US interest-rate differentials – a central feature of the projections – thereby moderating the momentum of the recovery.

In these conditions, reducing budget deficits is crucial to the achievement of better economic performance in the medium run. As in other OECD countries, consolidation efforts made during the cyclical upswing in the 1980s have proved insufficient to restore control over the fiscal situation. With weak economic activity in recent years, and despite corrective fiscal action, the general government deficit has reached a new record level of 7 per cent of GDP. As a result, the net public debt-to-GDP ratio has grown sharply and, at over 60 per cent of GDP, now exceeds the OECD average by a wide margin. The counterpart of rapid public-debt accumulation has been a run of large current-account deficits and rising external debt. These developments have left the economy vulnerable to changes in financial-market sentiment, contributing to short-term interest rate volatility and high long-term credit costs.

The new Government that took office in late 1993 has assigned priority to putting federal finances on a sound basis. Accordingly, in the February 1994 Budget, the authorities took action to curtail spending (through cuts in defence expenditure, reductions in unemployment-insurance benefits, and the extension of wage freezes for government employees) and – to a much lesser extent – to strengthen revenue (by broadening the tax base). Together with the effects of continued economic expansion and savings expected from reform of Canada's social-security system, these measures are expected to reduce the federal budget deficit from over 6 per cent of GDP in 1993/94 to about 3 per cent in 1996/97 – the interim target set by the Government on the road to the complete elimination of the deficit.

While this objective appears ambitious in so far as it would bring down the federal deficit-to-GDP ratio to a level not reached since the mid-1970s, its achievement would still imply the persistence of a significant structural imbalance as well as a further rise in the debt-to-GDP ratio. Moreover, the deficit reduction envisaged in the current fiscal year is relatively modest, with larger declines projected further down the road. Such a fiscal outlook has raised concerns in financial markets, as evidenced by the recent rise in Canada/US interest-rate differentials. Against this background, therefore, it would seem desirable to take advantage of the strengthening recovery to accelerate budget consolidation, with a view to stopping the rise in the debt-to-GDP ratio and achieving a sustainable fiscal position. In any case, the strict minimum required to restore financial-market confidence after several years of fiscal slippage would be to meet the deficit targets as set out in the February 1994 Budget, even if this should necessitate additional consolidation measures to offset the adverse effect of higher-than-expected interest rates on debt servicing costs. In this regard, it is important that every effort be made to secure budget savings from the announced social-security reform.

The fiscal outlook appears even more difficult if the sizeable budget deficits of the provinces are taken into account. Indeed, developments at the provincial level represent a large part of the deterioration in public finances in the early 1990s. With concerns about the rapid rise in provincial debt leading to a number of credit downgradings by rating agencies, provinces moved to a restrictive policy stance in 1993, and now all have plans to balance their budget in the medium run. However, in most cases further adjustment measures will be required to achieve that target. In particular, provincial finances are likely to be affected by recent interest-rate increases and the federal government's intentions to restrain certain social-security transfers from 1995. Although much of the provinces' fiscal problem is due to the expansionary policies they followed early in the 1990s, the federal government's efforts to contain transfers to them have also played a role. It is therefore important that the reform of social programmes now being considered be undertaken in a co-ordinated manner, with a view to generating fiscal savings for the public sector as a whole rather than specific levels of government.

Progress in fiscal consolidation would greatly facilitate the operation of monetary policy, which has aimed at encouraging reductions in interest rates consistent with declining inflation pressures. With the introduction of official inflation-reduction targets in 1991, monetary policy has contributed to lowering inflation and inflation expectations significantly. Indeed, consumer-price increases – adjusted for one-off factors such as large indirect-tax changes – have been consistently close to the lower end of the official target band. However, high risk premia built into Canadian interest rates have prevented the economy from fully reaping the benefits of a low-inflation environment. Indeed, *real* long-term interest rates have hardly declined in recent years and now are among the highest in the OECD area. Hence the necessity for more rapid fiscal consolidation to alleviate the pressure on long-term rates at a time when, after having eased substantially since 1990, monetary conditions have tended to tighten somewhat, as short-term interest rates have risen significantly in response to the fall of the exchange rate.

The recent agreement between the new Government and the Bank of Canada to maintain the objective of holding inflation inside the range of 1 to 3 per cent from 1995 to 1998 should further bolster policy credibility. However, the real test in this regard will come as the economy approaches full capacity. Against this, persistently high real interest rates due to non-monetary factors could undermine the public support for the policy framework. Moreover, while the inflation targets have been useful in making explicit the authorities' ultimate policy objectives, they provide no guidelines as to how these are to be achieved. More transparency in this respect – for instance, the publication of a detailed assessment of the inflation outlook – might help guide market expectations and thereby strengthen the effectiveness of monetary policy.

Structural policies are also a key to better economic performance in the medium term. So far, the major structural reforms implemented since the mid-1980s have been slow in producing the expected gains in economic efficiency and growth potential. Although this appears to reflect the substantial short-run costs associated with the adjustment to a more competitive environment, it may also suggest the existence of remaining impediments to faster output and employment growth. With a view to identifying these, the new Government is currently undertaking a number of comprehensive structural-policy reviews, encompassing in particular the social-security system. In addition, it has already taken measures to reform the unemployment-insurance system, enhance job training, support small businesses, and promote technological innovation, while continuing the previous administration's policy of trade liberalisation by signing the North American Free Trade Agreement (NAFTA) as well as the Uruguay Round agreement.

Areas where further reforms would be particularly useful include internal trade, agriculture, indirect taxation, and social security. Continuing progress towards reducing interprovincial trade barriers remains of utmost importance, since the recent intergovernmental Agreement on Internal Trade was less comprehensive than initially intended. Also, despite a significant reduction in agricultural support in recent years, sustained efforts will be needed to keep subsidies on a downward trend; in addition, distortions associated with Canada's supply-management system for certain agricultural commodities remain, although high tariffs will replace import restrictions under the Uruguay Round agreement. Moreover, it would be desirable that the forthcoming overhaul of the Goods and Services Tax (GST) bring about the much needed harmonisation of the ten different sales taxes now in place at the federal and provincial level. Finally, as discussed in detail in Part III of the Survey, there is considerable scope for further reforming the unemployment-insurance system and other social programmes, with a view both to reducing their distortionary effects on the economy and to securing fiscal savings.

Canada's income-security system is a complex mixture of programmes delivered by the federal, provincial and municipal governments. In addition to direct expenditures, the federal and provincial tax systems also contribute to achieving the goal of income security. In broad terms, the federal government administers most income-security benefits for seniors, families with children and the unemployed, in addition to contributing to the financing of social services and programmes of last resort which are administered by the provinces and some municipalities. The federal government also makes major contributions to funding post-secondary education and health care. Some features of the system – such as the lack of co-ordination between programmes, the generosity of benefits, and the emphasis on passive income support – reflect the fact that it evolved in a period of strong economic growth and low unemployment.

Given these features, Canada – like many other OECD countries – has experienced a trend rise in both the number of dependents and total expenditure on social programmes since the 1970s. Initially this reflected the introduction of new programmes as well as the expansion of coverage and benefits of existing ones. Subsequently – and in particular during the recessions of the early 1980s and early 1990s – some disconcerting demand-side characteristics have emerged: both average and long-term unemployment have risen markedly, the situation facing new entrants into the labour force has deteriorated, and – with more unevenly distributed household incomes and changing family structures – a larger proportion of the population has become reliant on transfer incomes.

In addition to these expenditure concerns, there is a growing consensus that the inherent incentive distortions of unemployment insurance (and income support more generally) can lead to a reverse situation where benefit provision tends to promote unemployment and welfare dependency. Empirical evidence, both for Canada and a number of other OECD countries, suggests that unemployment insurance encourages voluntary unemployment, promotes marginal attachment to the labour force by subsidising unstable and seasonal industries, and underpins high and rising payroll taxes which further deter both labour demand and supply. In turn, these disincentives to labour-force participation and investment in human capital result in a lower economic growth potential. Specific features of the Canadian unemployment-insurance system tend to reinforce these distortions. They include regional variations in the generosity of benefits (depending on the unemployment rate), the absence of experience rating, a lack of co-ordination with provincial welfare programmes, and a relatively high amount of expenditure on passive income support. Despite these problems, there are substantial benefits associated with unemployment insurance; in particular, it partly relieves people who have lost their job from immediate financial concerns, thereby facilitating more efficient job search and acting as a countercyclical force in the economy.

With regard to social assistance, there is evidence in Canada that – though successful in reducing poverty and inequality – income support promotes and prolongs welfare dependency. This is not surprising given that the system was originally developed for "unemployable" individuals while "employable" people receiving welfare are now almost a majority. A major concern is the existence of "welfare traps", where the net financial return to entering the labour force is significantly reduced by the high implicit tax rates resulting from the loss of both benefits and access to welfare services. Such traps can also promote longer-term welfare dependence. Indeed, the likelihood of repeat users leaving welfare tends to decline with each successive period they receive assistance.

In addressing these problems, any attempt to reform the current income-security system must involve changes to unemployment-insurance provision, given its relative importance as well as its interaction with other social programmes. Such interaction means that a co-ordinated reform process amongst all levels of government would be appropriate. With regard to unemployment insurance, three main avenues of reform appear important: less regional differentiation of benefits, adoption of some sort of experience rating and greater use of active labour-market programmes. Although progress has already been made in these areas, further reform appears necessary. The Government has recently taken initiatives to this effect, with a taskforce due to deliver some options for public debate in late-1994. This represents an attempt to co-ordinate changes at both the federal and provincial government levels, with a view to improving the interactions between unemployment insurance and the various provincial social-security schemes.

As for social assistance, current design issues include better integration with unemployment insurance, increased efforts to enhance the school-to-work transition, and greater focus on improving the employability and earnings potential of individuals. Some progress has been made in all three areas, with several provincial experiments currently under way. These usually include some form of wage subsidy for on-the-job training, job-search assistance, educational or vocational training, and public-sector employment programmes. Provinces are also increasingly experimenting with different forms of "negative income tax" systems, which lower the marginal tax rate associated with leaving welfare and entering the labour force. Such programmes appear critical to raising work incentives while providing a means of better integrating federal and provincial government roles in welfare provision (primarily through the expanded use of child tax benefits). However, care should be taken to ensure that lower taxes for certain groups of individuals do not imply dramatic income-tax increases elsewhere. Instead, any tax rises required to keep tax changes revenue-neutral overall should be applied to the broadest possible alternative tax bases.

The recently-announced reform process launched by the federal government could go considerably further than incremental changes to the unemployment-insurance and social-assistance programmes. It opens the possibility of looking at these programmes, not in isolation, but as to how they work together, including their combined impact on the various regions of the country. At the same time, it provides the opportunity to review such programmes not only in terms of their role in income security, but also as part of a broader human-resources development strategy encompassing learning, social services, employability, and child care.

In summary, the Canadian economy is now growing at a robust pace, with increased domestic spending reinforcing export demand. The basic economic conditions for sustained growth are in place, including a low-inflation environment, restored international competitiveness, and strong business capital spending. However, concerns about budgetary developments and the future of the federation have made the economy vulnerable to financial-market disturbances, as evidenced by recurrent exchange-rate weakness and subsequent upward pressures on interest rates despite the favourable inflation performance. Even if temporary, such pressures could affect confidence and hold back activity in interest-sensitive sectors of the economy. Progress in fiscal consolidation – both federal and provincial – remains therefore of primary importance in order to reduce the current high risk premium built into Canadian interest rates and thereby limit possible adverse effects on investment and activity. Medium-term performance also needs to be supported by further structural reforms, in particular in areas such as internal trade barriers and work-disincentives associated with the income-support system.

Notes

1. According to a special GALLUP Survey.

2. Revised statistics show that the growth in the population resident in Canada has displayed larger swings than earlier thought. This is because the number of non-permanent residents – also a source of demographic requirements for housing – rose sharply in the late 1980s, partly due to an influx of refugee claimants, and has subsequently declined to a more normal level. It is nonetheless likely that immigrants – especially refugee claimants – have lower effective demand for housing for some time.

3. Diagram 20 in Part III offers an illustration of this point.

4. Recent estimates point to a "natural rate" of unemployment in the 8½ to 10 per cent range. With structural reforms tending to reduce the "natural rate", its apparent upward shift in recent years can probably be attributed to hysteresis effects emanating from the recession of the early 1990s, which will tend to reverse themselves as labour markets improve. Thus, a higher "natural rate" is unlikely to become a constraint to non-inflationary growth in the foreseeable future.

5. Statistics Canada, Public sector assets and liabilities, historical overview.

6. For a detailed discussion see the OECD Economic Surveys of Canada 1992 and 1993 as well as the Bank of Canada Reviews March and September 1991.

7. Bank of Canada Review, March 1991.

8. Duguay, Pierre, "Empirical Evidence of the Strength of the Monetary Transmission Mechanism in Canada: An Aggregate Approach", *Journal of Monetary Economics*, 33 (1994).

9. See Crow, John W., "Monetary Policy under a Floating Exchange Rate Regime: the Canadian Experience", Lecture at the Stockholm School of Economics, April 1993; and Bank of Canada Review, Spring 1994.

10. *I.e.* items in transit through the payment clearing system.

11. "Facing Choices Together: Response to pre-Budget consultations", Government of Canada (February 1994).

12. Card and Freeman (1993) claim that by leaning against the wind, Canada managed to lower poverty rates during a decade when slow economic growth and structural economic and social change. Simulations by Blank and Hanratty suggest that if the United States had adopted Canada's welfare policies, it would have avoided the trend of rising child poverty. Blackburn and Bloom's analyses show that Canada's income transfer system played a major

role in keeping family income inequality from rising, while Card and Riddell's analysis of unemployment compensation suggests that the unemployment insurance system encouraged some persons with limited skills and labour force attachment to continue working just enough to maintain eligibility.

13. However, some programmes, such as unemployment insurance, contain features of more than one of these categories.

14. There is no single commonly used definition of "income security"; the boundaries employed in Table 9 are those used by Statistics Canada. Narrower definitions would exclude items such as employment and training programmes, while broader definitions would include health programmes. In this chapter, the term "social security" refers to the broad set of programmes covering income security and health. It must also be noted that the figures in Table 9 understate total expenditure on income security in the sense that they do not include tax expenditures nor do they include income security provided by employers, in the form of non-wage benefits, or by the voluntary sector. Because the benefits received from programmes such as unemployment insurance, OAS and CPP/QPP are taxable, and because of the "clawback" of OAS and UI benefits for higher income recipients, net expenditures on income security are less than gross expenditures. See Battle and Torjman (1993a) for information on the magnitudes of gross and net expenditures on income security in Canada.

15. For an analysis of the Child Tax Benefit and the programmes it replaced, see Kesselman (1993).

16. Only social assistance and social services remain cost-shared between the federal and provincial governments under the Canada Assistance Plan (CAP). The federal government's funding contribution for health and post-secondary education, which was previously based on a 50-50 cost-share arrangement, is now provided in the form of block funding, *i.e.* it is independent of the amount spent by the province on those activities.

17. The definitions of "unemployed employables" vary among provinces. "Unemployables" incorporates, for example, individuals who are disabled, lone-parents (depending on the province), students, foster children and the aged.

18. The economic efficiency rationale for publicly provided unemployment insurance is discussed in Green and Riddell (1993a).

19. See Dingledine (1981) for a detailed chronology of the evolution of UI in Canada from 1940 to 1980. For more recent information see Statistics Canada (1984), Green and Riddell (1993a) and Battle and Tjorman (1993b).

20. Benefits received from the UI, CPP/QPP and OAS programmes are taxable. In addition there is a clawback of UI and OAS benefits received by high income recipients. In the case of UI, claimants whose net yearly income, including UI benefits, is more than 1.5 times the maximum insurable income (C$ 60 840 in 1994), must pay back 30 per cent of the benefits over that limit.

21. Since that time the principal exclusions from coverage have been the self-employed, those over 65 years of age, those with very low earnings, and those working less than 15 hours per week. Approximately 90 per cent of the labour force is covered.

22. This has been the case for most social programmes. See Battle and Tjorman (1993b).

23. Under the most recent provisions, as noted in the text, employment of as little as 12 weeks in a maximum entitlement region qualifies the claimant for up to 50 weeks of benefits. However, in order to qualify for the maximum benefit duration of 50 weeks, 44 weeks of employment are required.

24. Ten weeks from the "previous employment phase" and 32 from the "regional extended benefit phase".

25. Prior to the 1990 changes to the Act, the programme was funded by employer and employee contributions and the federal government. In 1989, the federal government contributed C$ 2.9 billion out of expenditures of C$ 12.6 billion.

26. The 1971 UI Act allowed for experience rating. However, that provision was never implemented and was subsequently removed.

27. However, since 1990 the growth in the federal government's share of social assistance expenditures in Alberta, British Columbia and Ontario (the three wealthiest provinces) has been limited to 5 per cent per year. As a consequence, the federal share of welfare expenditures in British Columbia and Ontario has fallen substantially below 50 per cent, while Alberta has kept the federal share at 50 per cent by reducing social assistance costs through case load and benefit reductions.

28. See Blank and Hanratty (1993) for a comparison of Canadian and US benefit levels.

29. In what follows the terms welfare or social assistance are used interchangeably to refer to the combination of social services and social assistance.

30. These data incorporate provincial and local government expenditures on social assistance and social services as well as federal expenditures for registered Indians.

31. The following is based on Barrett (1994) and Cragg (1994).

32. Canada was not unique in this respect. In the analysis of social expenditure growth in the OECD countries during the period 1960-81 (OECD, 1985), it was concluded that the main source of growth was discretionary policy decisions to increase benefit levels and expand coverage. Demographic factors were relatively unimportant.

33. However, this is to some extent a short-run concern, given that a higher capital intensity raises labour productivity, and potentially employment levels.

34. Caution should be taken when using such comparisons. For example, no account is taken of private expenditure, which is very significant in the United States.

35. Using a definition of three or more claims in five years for repeat users, about 38 per cent of Canada's claimant population were repeaters between 1986 and 1991. In Atlantic Canada, roughly 60 per cent of all claimants were repeat users under the same definition.

36. Green and Riddell (1993b) find that individuals working 10 to 13 weeks in 1989 (i.e. enough to meet the entrance requirement) tend to work much longer hours when they do work than is the case for other workers.

37. See Winer and Gauthier (1982) and Vanderkamp (1986) for further analysis and evidence in the Canadian setting.

38. In the absence of UI, industries with unstable employment would have to pay a wage premium to attract workers while industries with stable employment would face lower

labour costs. These differences in labour costs feed through to output prices and thus the relative size of the industry in terms of output and employment.

39. See Anderson and Meyer (1993), Card and Levine (1991), and Topel (1983). Topel (1983) estimates that incomplete experience rating may account for as much as 30 per cent of all temporary layoffs. Card and Levine (1991) estimate that incomplete experience rating accounts for 50 per cent of temporary layoff unemployment during cyclical downturns.

40. See, for example, Kroeger (1994). Organisations representing small business have been the most vocal opponents of rising payroll taxes.

41. The employee premium rate for 1995 will not be raised to C\$ 3.30 of insurable earnings, as required by the UI Act, but rolled back to their 1993 level of C\$ 3.00 (from C\$ 3.07 at present).

42. In the absence of reforms to the existing Canada and Quebec Pension Plans and to workers' compensation programmes, payroll taxes are projected to rise significantly in the future.

43. See Kesselman (1994) for an analysis of provincial payroll taxes in Canada.

44. With regard to labour supply, taxes alter the trade-off between work and leisure, promoting both an "income" and "substitution" effect. The income effect supposes that, given that increased taxes lower disposable incomes, more labour will be supplied to maintain a constant consumption wage. The substitution effect, however, suggests that increased taxes will lower labour supply as the opportunity cost of leisure has declined. However, although the effect on labour supply may be ambiguous, any rise in labour costs due to tax increases – which depends on relative wage flexibility – will unambiguously lower the labour demand schedule.

45. This is relevant in determining unemployment given that employers will generally demand labour according to their marginal value of output relative to their wage costs, while employees will supply labour according to the level of consumption they can finance out of the earned income.

46. In this respect it can be shown that, by shifting the incidence of tax – in a revenue neutral fashion – from labour onto a wider based consumption tax, in a high wage resistant country such as Canada positive benefits can accrue for employment levels.

47. See Canadian Labour Market and Productivity Centre (1990, Table 4) and Human Resources Development Canada (1994). Note that the definition of "employable" varies by province and in some provinces has changed over time.

48. The increase in inequality in employment income has been much greater than the increase in inequality in total income, reflecting the importance of transfer income in preventing what would otherwise have been a substantial rise in absolute poverty. Recent analysis of changing income inequality in Canada is provided by Morissette, Myles and Picot (1993).

49. Such "traps" have been identified for low-income earners in Canada, the United Kingdom, Australia, New Zealand and many European countries. Indeed, OECD countries operate a complex menu of social assistance benefits, with a variety of benefit reduction rates in response to earned income. In general, these benefit reduction rates are often zero for child benefits, intermediate for housing benefits, and often around 100 per cent for unemployment benefits.

50. These include for example: the Commission of Inquiry on UI (1986); Royal Commission on Employment and Unemployment, Newfoundland (1986); and the Royal Commission on the Economic Union and Development Prospects (1985).

51. Primarily in the manufacturing and resource sectors for youths entering the labour force with limited education and skills.

52. The proportion of the unemployed who are unemployed six months or longer rose from about 15 per cent in the 1976-81 period to about 24 per cent during 1982-87. Although this proportion declined to about 20 per cent as the economy reached a cyclical peak in 1988-90, it has subsequently risen sharply and currently stands at over 30 per cent.

53. The decline in Canada's youth population in the 1980s was the largest among OECD countries. During that decade, the labour market situation for youths – as measured by the unemployment rate, labour force participation rate, and employment-to-population ratio – improved, despite the 1981-82 recession.

54. Both the Royal Commission on the Economic Union and Development Prospects for Canada (1985) and the Commission of Inquiry on Unemployment Insurance (1986) recommended sweeping changes to UI as part of a package of income security reforms.

55. Prior to these changes, individuals were entitled to one week of benefits for each week of work up to a maximum, while additional weeks of work carried a lower benefit entitlement (one week of benefits for each two weeks of work). In high-unemployment regions, only the initial phase was relevant because the upper limit of 50 weeks of benefits was reached with only 18 weeks of previous work experience.

56. This may, for example, result in an income effect reducing work incentives.

57. For example, empirical work suggests that higher marginal tax rates for high-income earners are likely to have less effect on their work effort than on low income individuals. Sadka et al. (1980) estimate that individuals in the bottom income quintile have an elasticity of hours worked with respect to the net wage rate of 0.26, compared to 0.10 for the top income quintile.

58. For example, the Royal Commission on the Economic Union and Development Prospects for Canada, 1985.

59. The maximum supplement is C$ 500 per annum and the supplement is phased out when family earnings reach about C$ 26 000 (Kesselman, 1993).

60. A description of the Quebec approach is provided by Bouchard (1993). Because the minimum wage and other factors affecting market income are associated with individuals, yet social assistance benefits are based on family size and composition, achieving work incentives for different types of families requires an income supplementation system based on family size and composition, which is integrated with the tax system.

Bibliography

Advisory Council on Adjustment (1989) *Adjusting to Win*. Ottawa: Minister of Supply and Services.

Allen, Douglas W. (1993) "Welfare and the Family: The Canadian Experience" *Journal of Labor Economics 11* (January) S201-S223.

Anderson, Patricia M. and Bruce D. Meyer (1993) "Unemployment Insurance in the United States: Layoff Incentives and Cross Subsidies" *Journal of Labor Economics 11* (January) S70-S95.

Atkinson, Anthony B., J. Gomulka, John Micklewright and N. Rau (1984) "Unemployment Benefit, Duration and Incentives in Britain: How Robust Is the Evidence?" *Journal of Public Economics 23*, 3-26.

Atkinson, A.B. (1987), "Income Maintenance and Social Insurance" in Auerbach, A.J. and M. Feldstein (ed.), Handbook of Public Economics Volume II, Amsterdam: North Holland, pp. 779-908.

Baker, Michael and Samuel A. Rea, Jr (1993), "Employment Spells and Unemployment Insurance Eligibility Requirements", mimeo, Univeristy, Toronto.

Barrett, Garry (1994), "The Duration of Income Assistance Spells in British Columbia", paper presented at CERF Workshop on Labour Markets and Income Support, Vancouver, B.C.

Battle, Ken and Sherri Torjman (1993*a*), *Opening the Books on Social Spending*. Ottawa: The Caledon Institute of Social Policy.

Battle, Ken and Sherri Torjman (1993*b*), *Federal Social* programme*s: Setting the Record Straight*. Ottawa: The Caledon Institute of Social Policy.

Battle, Ken and Sherri Torjman (1993*c*), *The Welfare Wall: The Interaction of the Welfare and Tax Systems*. Ottawa: The Caledon Institute of Social Policy.

Betcherman, Gordon and Rene Morissette (1993), "Recent Youth Labour Market Experiences in Canada" paper presented at Canadian Employment Research Forum workshop on Youth Labour Adjustment, June 1993.

Blank, Rebecca M. and Maria J. Hanratty (1993), "Responding to Need: A Comparison of Social Safety Nets in Canada and the United States" in David Card and Richard B. Freeman (eds.) *Small Differences That Matter: Labor Markets and Income Maintenance in Canada and the United States*. Chicago: University of Chicago Press and NBER.

Bouchard, Genevieve (1993), "Provincial perspective: Quebec" in Elisabeth B. Reynolds ed. *Income Security in Canada: Changing Needs, Changing Means.* Montreal: Institute for Research on Public Policy.

Canadian Labour Market and Productivity Centre (1990), *Report of the CLMPC Task Force on the Labour Force Development Strategy.* Ottawa: CLMPC.

Card, David and W. Craig Riddell (1993), "A Comparative Analysis of Unemployment in Canada and the United States" in *Small Differences That Matter: Labor Markets and Income Maintenance in Canada and the United States,* edited by David Card and Richard B. Freeman. Chicago: University of Chicago Press and National Bureau of Economic Research.

Card, David and Richard B. Freeman (1993), *Small Differences That Matter: Labor Markets and Income Maintenance in Canada and the United States.* Chicago: University of Chicago Press and NBER.

Card, David and Phillip B. Levine (1991), "Unemployment Insurance Taxes and the Cyclical Properties of Employment and Unemployment" Princeton University, Industrial Relations Section, Working Paper No. 288.

Christofides, Louis N. and Chris J. McKenna (1993), "Employment Flows and Job Tenure in Canada", *Canadian Public Policy 29* (June) 145-161.

Coe, D.T. (1990), "Structural Determinants of the Natural Rate of Unemployment in Canada", IMF Staff Papers, Vol. 37, No. 1, pp. 94-115.

Commission of Inquiry on Unemployment Insurance (1986), *Report.* Ottawa: Supply and Services.

Corak, Miles (1992), "The Duration of Unemployment Insurance Payments" Economic Council of Canada Working Paper No. 42. Ottawa: Economic Council of Canada.

Corak, Miles (1993), "Unemployment Insurance Once Again: The Incidence of Repeat Participation in the Canadian UI programme" *Canadian Public Policy 19* (June) 162-76.

Corak, Miles (1994), "Unemployment Insurance, Work Disincentives, and the Canadian Labour Market: An Overview" in *Unemployment Insurance: How to Make It Work.* Toronto: C.D. Howe Institute.

Cousineau, Jean-Michel (1985), "Unemployment Insurance and Labour Market Adjustments" in *Income Distribution and Economic Security in Canada,* edited by Francois Vaillancourt. Toronto: University of Toronto Press.

Cragg, Michael (1994), "The Dynamics of Welfare Participation in British Columbia", paper presented at CERF Workshop on Labour Markets and Income Support, Vancouver, B.C.

Dingledine, Gary (1981), *A Chronology of Response: The Evolution of Unemployment Insurance from 1940 to 1980.* Ottawa: Minister of Supply and Services.

Economic Council of Canada (1991), *Employment in the Service Economy.* Ottawa: Ministry of Supply and Services.

Employment and Immigration Canada (1989), *Success in the Works: A Labour Force Development Strategy for Canada.* Ottawa: Employment and Immigration Canada.

Employment and Immigration Canada (1992), *Canadian Jobs Strategy Evaluation Outcomes: Lessons Learned.* programme Evaluation Branch, Ottawa.

131

Employment and Immigration Canada (1993), *Evaluation of Employability Initiatives for Social Assistance Recipients.* Ottawa: programme Evaluation Branch, EIC.

Fortin, Bernard (1985), "Income Security in Canada" in F. Vaillancourt (ed.) *Income Distribution and Economic Security in Canada.* Toronto: University of Toronto Press, pp. 153-86.

Garfinkel, Irwin, Sara S. McLanahan and Philip K. Robins, eds. (1992), *Child Support Assurance.* Washington D.C.: The Urban Institute.

Green, David A. and W. Craig Riddell (1993*a*), "The Economic Effects of Unemployment Insurance in Canada: An Empirical Analysis of UI Disentitlement" *Journal of Labor Economics 11* (January) S96-S147.

Green, David A. and W. Craig Riddell (1993*b*), "Qualifying for Unemployment Insurance: An Empirical Analysis" Department of Economics, University of British Columbia, Discussion Paper 93-33.

Ham, John C., and Samuel A. Rea, Jr. (1987), "Unemployment Insurance and Male Unemployment Duration in Canada". *Journal of Labor Economics 5* (July) 325-53.

Health and Welfare Canada (1985), *Social Security Statistics: Canada and Provinces 1958-59 to 1982-83.* Ottawa: Health and Welfare Canada.

Health and Welfare Canada (1988), *Social Security Statistics: Canada and Provinces 1963-64 to 1987-88.* Ottawa: Health and Welfare Canada.

Hobson, Paul A. and France St-Hilaire (1993), "Fiscal Transfers and the Federal Role in Income Security" in Elisabeth B. Reynolds (ed.) *Income Security in Canada: Changing Needs, Changing Means.* Montreal: Institute for Research on Public Policy, 117-147.

Human Resources Development Canada (1994*a*), *Proposed Changes to the Unemployment Insurance* programme. Ottawa: HRD.

Human Resources Development Canada (1994*b*), *Social Security in Canada.* Ottawa: HRD.

Kaliski, Stephan (1985), "Trends, Changes and Imbalances: A Survey of the Canadian Labour Market" in *Work and Pay: The Canadian Labour Market*, edited by W. Craig Riddell. Toronto: University of Toronto Press.

Kesselman, Jonathan R. (1983), *Financing Canadian Unemployment Insurance.* Toronto: Canadian Tax Foundation.

Kesselman, Jonathan R. (1992), "Income Security via the Tax System: Canadian and American Reforms" in J. Shoven and J. Whalley (eds.) *Canada-US Tax Comparisons.* Chicago: University of Chicago Press and NBER, pp. 97-150.

Kesselman, Jonathan R. (1993), "The Child Tax Benefit: Simple, Fair Responsive?" *Canadian Public Policy/Analyse de Politiques 19* (June) 109-132.

Kesselman, Jonathan R. (1994), "Canadian Provincial Payroll Taxation: A Structural and Policy Analysis" Department of Economics, University of British Columbia, Discussion Paper 94-07.

Kesselman, Jonathan R. and W. Craig Riddell (1991), "Assessment of Alternative Subsidy Treatments for the EIC Self-Sufficiency Project" study prepared for the Innovations programme, Employment and Immigration Canada.

Kroeger, Arthur (1994), "Governments and the 'Jobs' Issue". The Eric John Hansen Memorial Lecture, Department of Economics, University of Alberta, Edmonton, Alberta.

Layard, P., S. Nickell and R. Jackman (1991), "Unemployment: Macroeconomic Performance and the Labour Market", Oxford University Press.

Meyer, Bruce. D. (1992), "Policy Lessons from the US Unemployment Insurance Experiments", Working Paper, Department of Economics, Northwestern University.

Meyer, Daniel R., Irwin Garfinkel, Judi Bartfield and Pat Brown (1994), "Child Support Reform in Wisconsin: From Proposals to Implementation to Evaluation" paper presented at Canadian Employment Research Forum workshop on Labour Markets and Income Support, Vancouver, March 1994.

Milbourne, Ross D., Douglas D. Purvis and David Scoones (1991), "Unemployment Insurance and Unemployment Dynamics". *Canadian Journal of Economics 24* (November) 804-26.

Ministry of Social Services, Province of British Columbia (1992), *Routes to Independence: The Effectiveness of Employment and Training* programme*s for Income Assistance Recipients in British Columbia.* Victoria, B.C.: Research, Evaluation and Statistics Branch, Ministry of Social Services.

Moorthy, Vivek (1989-90), "Unemployment in Canada and the United States: The Role of Unemployment Insurance Benefits". *Federal Reserve Bank of New York Quarterly Review 14* (Winter) 48-61.

Morisette, Rene, John Myles and Garnett Picot (1993), "What is Happening to Earnings Inequality in Canada?" Statistics Canada, Analytical Studies Branch, Research Paper, December.

National Council of Welfare (1987), *Welfare in Canada: The Tangled Safety Net.* Ottawa: National Council of Welfare.

National Council of Welfare (1992), *Welfare Reform.* Ottawa: National Council of Welfare.

Organisation for Economic Co-operation and Development (1981), *The Welfare State in Crisis,* Paris.

Organisation for Economic Co-operation and Development (1985), *Social Expenditure 1960-1990: Problems of growth and control,* Paris.

Organisation for Economic Co-operation and Development (1988), "Description of Unemployment Benefit Systems in OECD Countries" *Employment Outlook,* Paris.

Organisation for Economic Co-operation and Development (1990a), *Labour Market Policies for the 1990s,* Paris.

Organisation for Economic Co-operation and Development (1990b), "Employer Versus Employee Taxation: The Impact on Employment", *Employment Outlook,* Paris.

Organisation for Economic Co-operation and Development (1991), "Unemployment Benefit Rules and Labour Market Policy", *Economic Outlook,* Paris.

Organisation for Economic Co-operation and Development (1993), "Active Labour Market Policies: Assessing Macroeconomic and Microeconomic Effects", *Employment Outlook,* Paris.

Organisation for Economic Co-operation and Development (1994), "Employment/Unemployment Study Draft Background Report", Chapters 4, 7 and 8, Paris.

Phipps, Shelley (1993), "Does Unemployment Insurance Increase Unemployment?" *Canadian Business Economics 1* (Spring) 37-50.

Royal Commission on Employment and Unemployment, Newfoundland and Labrador (1986), *Report*. St. Johns, Newfoundland: Royal Commission on Employment and Unemployment.

Royal Commission on the Economic Union and Development Prospects for Canada (1985), *Report*. Ottawa: Supply and Services.

Sadka, E., I. Garfinkel and K. Moreland (1982), "Income Testing and Social Welfare", in Garfinkel (ed.) "Income tested transfer programs", New York Academic Press.

Sarlo, C. (1992), "Poverty in Canada", The Fraser Institute, Vancouver, Canada.

Setterfield, M. A., D. V. Gordon and L. Osberg (1992), "Searching for a Will O' the Wisp: An Empirical Study of the NAIRU in Canada", *European Economic Review 36*, 119-36.

Statistics Canada (1984), *Social Security National* programmes. Vol. 2: *Unemployment Insurance*. Ottawa: Ministry of Supply and Services.

Topel, Robert (1983), "On Layoffs and Unemployment Insurance" *American Economic Review 73*, 541-59.

Vanderkamp, John (1986), "The Efficiency of the Interregional Adjustment Process", in *Disparities and Interregional Adjustment* edited by Kenneth Norrie. Toronto: University of Toronto Press.

Williams, B (1994), "Unemployment Insurance and Labour Market Distortions", ESPAD, Ministry of Finance, Canada.

Wines, Stanley L. and D. Gautier (1982), *Internal Migration and Fiscal Structure*. Ottawa: Economic Council, Canada.

Labour market impacts of Unemployment Insurance and payroll taxes

Work disincentives of the Unemployment Insurance system

By altering the incentives facing workers and firms, unemployment insurance (UI) and payroll taxes can influence decisions on labour supply, job search, layoffs, and inter-regional mobility. Indeed, across OECD countries, there is evidence that unemployment benefits can prolong the length of a recession by affecting both the level and duration of unemployment. It also appears that entitlements to unemployment benefits can partially explain the differences across countries in the structure of unemployment by age, sex and duration. Furthermore, rising payroll taxes can lower employment and raise unemployment in economies with wage rigidity. This annex provides a summary of relevant empirical work in these fields, both across OECD countries and specific to Canada.

Cross-country evidence

Recent empirical work (largely summarised from OECD, 1994, Chapter 7) which searches for linkages between UI and unemployment gives attention to changes in benefits and unemployment over time across OECD countries. Diagram A1 displays summary benefit replacement rates since 1961 across several countries. Using this data it can be shown that during both the 1974-1975 and 1980-1982 recessions, it was the already high-benefit countries (Canada inclusive) which experienced the largest increase in unemployment. This correlation is further supported in the late-1980s and early-1990s by the experience of the Nordic countries. On an individual country basis, it is also noticeable that Canada, after the 1970s, experienced a consistently higher unemployment rate than the United States, coinciding with a rise in the replacement rate, despite having similar unemployment profiles during the 1950s and 1960s.

More formally, abstracting from cyclical influences, cross country regression analysis suggests an elasticity of around 1 per cent between changes in benefit replacement rates and unemployment, albeit with a considerable lag (OECD, 1994, Chapter 7). Indeed, this correlation may be stronger if account was taken of taxation and housing benefits, and recipients' previous work experience, as individuals with only a very short, or no, work experience are not included in the estimates. In sum, changes to the benefit systems in OECD countries since the 1960s are relevant when explaining developments in unemployment rates.

Diagram A1. **SUMMARY MEASURES OF BENEFIT ENTITLEMENTS**[1]

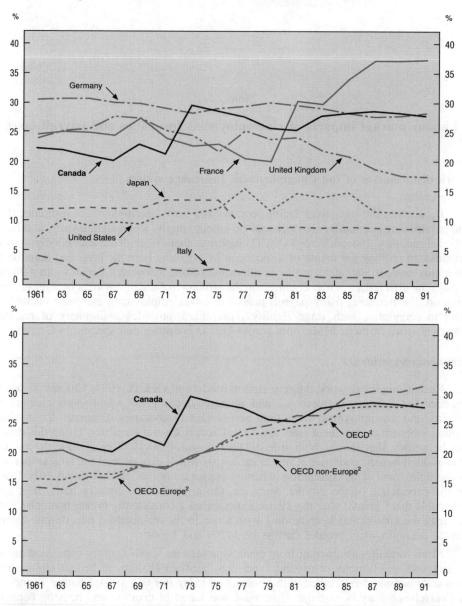

1. Average of the unemployment benefit replacement rates for two earnings, three family situations and three durations of unemployment.
2. Unweighted average.
Source: OECD (1994).

The claim that the level of benefit replacement rates and unemployment are linked is supported by correlations between the distribution of total unemployment by age, sex, household situation and the relative generosity of benefit entitlements of these groups across OECD countries. Diagram A2 highlights the positive correlation between the ratio of total female/male unemployment and the relative unemployment duration, as well as the relative generosity of replacement rates across 18 countries. The cross-country statistics indicate that although relative benefit entitlements may be of limited importance as an influence on short-term unemployment rates and duration, they can be a significant determinant for periods of long term unemployment (over one year). Furthermore, a positive correlation also exists between UI duration and unemployment duration (OECD, 1991), although, this does not always imply causation. Canada, for example, provides a reverse possibility (from unemployment to benefit duration) given the existence of regional-specific increases in UI duration in response to the regional unemployment rate. Nevertheless, on a cross-country basis, this is offset by both Japan and France where UI duration has been shortened in response to rising unemployment.

With regards to the effects of benefit generosity on the age structure of unemployment, again cross-country evidence indicates a positive correlation, especially for older workers. This is despite the relationship being potentially weakened since older workers may opt for more lucrative early retirement or disability benefits. With regards to Canada, Green and Riddell (1993a) show that a decline in benefit eligibility amongst older workers in 1976 led to a significant decline in the number of elderly unemployed – to around one-third of its previous level. The age group correlation across countries with respect to youth unemployment is also weakened by the work experience requirements in several countries to qualify for unemployment insurance. However, in countries where eligibility criteria for unemployment insurance are only weakly related to past work experience, youth unemployment has grown significantly faster than adult rates.

Interesting trends also emerge across countries when examining the relationship between relative benefit levels and the total number of unemployed individuals (Table A1). In high-benefit countries the total number of benefit recipients is greater than the total labour force survey measure of unemployment, with the reverse true in low-benefit countries. This suggests that the impact of benefits on the number of beneficiaries is greater than that on the labour force survey of unemployment. With regards to Canada, it is noteworthy that the beneficiary/unemployment ratio is significantly higher than in the United States. This can be explained by both the higher actual level of unemployment and the subsequent higher benefit entitlement. However, this ratio has fallen significantly in Canada in recent years.

Changes to benefit administration also appear important in determining the final level of benefit recipients and actual employment structure. Cross-country correlations suggest that effective benefit administration can significantly reduce many of the disincentive effects inherent in benefit entitlements. This is especially important given that only a limited proportion of the long-term unemployed are fully available for existing jobs – at least to the point they should be according to the relevant benefit legislation.[1] Nevertheless, introducing more effective benefit controls can prove difficult, with the result sometimes counterintuitive. In Canada, for example, the UI disqualification period for job quitters was increased from 6 to 12 weeks and the benefit replacement rate was

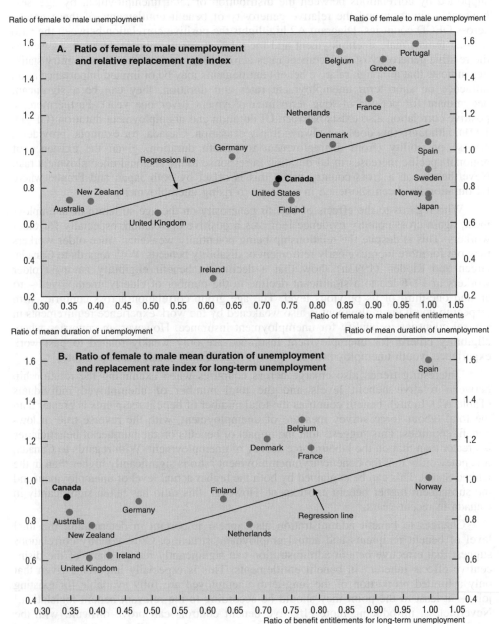

Diagram A2. **CHARACTERISTICS OF FEMALE AND MALE UNEMPLOYMENT RELATIVE TO BENEFIT ENTITLEMENTS**

Ratio of female to male unemployment

Ratio of female to male unemployment

A. Ratio of female to male unemployment and relative replacement rate index

Ratio of female to male benefit entitlements

Ratio of mean duration of unemployment

Ratio of mean duration of unemployment

B. Ratio of female to male mean duration of unemployment and replacement rate index for long-term unemployment

Ratio of benefit entitlements for long-term unemployment

Source: OECD (1994).

138

Table A.1. **Ratio of the number of unemployment beneficiaries[1] to the total number of unemployed**

	Date	Types of benefit covered[2]	Number of beneficiaries (000s)	Number of unemployed in labour force survey[3] (000s)	All beneficiaries as a percentage of LFS unemployment
Australia	1991	GI	666	812	82
Austria	1991	UI, UA	165	125	132
Belgium	1991	UI, GI	448	303	148
Canada	**1993**	**UI, GI**	**1 292**	**1 562**	**83**
Denmark	1992	UI, GI	313	277	113
Finland	1991	UI, GI	215	193	112
France	1991	UI, UA, GI	2 251	2 308	98
Germany	1990	UI, UA	1 291	1 451	89
Ireland	1989	UI, GI	220	206	107
Japan	1990	UI	482	1 340	36
Netherlands	1990	UI, GI	539	513	105
Norway	1991	UI	71	116	61
Spain	1992	UI, UA	1 633	2 774	59
Sweden	1988	UI, KAS	67	72	93
Switzerland	1991 Q2	UI	35	65	53
United Kingdom	1990	UI, GI	1 432	2 009	71
United States	1990	UI	2 320	6 874	34

1. Unemployment beneficiaries are defined here as people receiving unemployment insurance benefits or assistance benefits who are officially assessed as being wholly unemployed (regardless of their labour force survey status). Among groups not included in principle are people receiving insurance or assistance benefits for other reasons (*e.g.* sickness or retirement) and people who have a part-time job but are receiving part-time unemployment benefit.
2. Types of benefit covered are coded by UI = unemployment insurance, UA = unemployment assistance (*i.e.* a means-tested extension of benefit for persons who previously qualified for UI), GI = guaranteed income (means-tested minimum income), KAS = Sweden's "cash" (non-contributory but limited duration) benefit.
3. Labour force survey unemployed refers to unemployment reported from the Mikrocensus in the case of Austria.
Source: OECD (1994).

reduced from 60 to 50 per cent in 1990. More importantly, voluntarily quitting a job without just cause can now completely exclude an individual from benefits. However, doubt remains as to whether quitting is correctly reported, with lay-offs being negotiated instead. The United States example of "experience rating" severance payments is one means of minimising this problem, whereby employers who are unable to prove that a job separation was voluntary are liable for the whole UI cost of the lay-off.[2]

Country specific evidence

In relation to the effects of changes in unemployment benefits insurance on unemployment levels, the elasticities suggested by the cross-country research appear higher than indicated by previous individual country microeconomic analysis. With regards to the impact of individuals' replacement rates on unemployment duration, estimated elasticities are in the range 0-1.0 (Atkinson, 1987) or 0.2-0.9 (Layard *et al.*, 1990). In comparing these generally lower individual country elasticities to the OECD Secretariat's cross-country estimates, one possible explanation for the difference is that the impact of benefit entitlements on unemployment works both through labour supply and labour demand channels, with the cross-country estimates better accounting for these.

Nevertheless, individual country experience also suggests high benefit entitlements may encourage short employment spells, voluntary job leaving, long-term unemployment, older-worker unemployment, and higher incidences of reported involuntary part-time employment and even disability. Examples of these various outcomes exist, for example, with regard to: the 1971 increase in generosity of the UI system in Canada, the introduction of the disability benefit in the Netherlands in 1967, the indefinite assistance benefit in Finland in 1972, unemployment benefits for part time workers in Belgium in 1983, and the guaranteed income benefit introduced in France in 1989. Although these are examples where extreme change occurred in the generosity of benefits, countries which underwent less dramatic increases in benefit entitlement also experienced similar patterns of change (see OECD, 1994).

Canadian evidence

Much of the recent research on the impact of changes to Canada's UI system has used micro data[3] to better identify the impacts of specific programme parameters, as well as to gain more precise measurements of these effects. However, it is important to realise that significant changes have occurred to the generosity of the UI system since these studies were undertaken. These include decreases in the benefit rate, disqualification of voluntary quitters, and increases to entrance requirements.

One body of UI research has investigated the impact of two key parameters – the benefit rate and the maximum duration of benefits – on the duration of job search [Ham and Rea (1987) and Corak (1992)]. These studies find that: the benefit rate has no impact on the duration of search for males but a strong effect for females; and both the state of aggregate demand and the maximum duration of benefits influence the duration of unemployment. With respect to the latter, there is some tendency for individuals to become increasingly likely to obtain employment as they approach exhaustion of benefit entitlement (this could occur because they search more intensively or become more willing to accept any available job), although the effect is not large.

These results suggest that reducing the benefit rate would cause females to obtain employment more quickly, but would not greatly affect the behaviour of males. Reducing the maximum benefit duration would encourage some claimants to find jobs more quickly, but for others would imply that benefits would be exhausted sooner, with the possible implication of increased use of social assistance.

The impact of UI on the duration of employment, and thus on the incidence of unemployment (or the flow from employment into unemployment) has also been examined. Kaliski (1985) found that the ratio of employed to unemployed job search rose sharply following the introduction in the late 1970s of a reduced benefit rate and tighter qualification requirements. This suggests that tighter UI benefit qualification requirements can increase job-search activity. Subsequently the qualification requirements in Canada have tightened significantly, from 8 to 10 weeks in the 1970s to 12 to 20 weeks now.

The impact of UI on employment duration is also related to its effect on labour force participation. Recent evidence suggests that some individuals and firms have responded to UI incentives. In their analysis of Canada-United States unemployment, Card and Riddell (1993) find a tendency for Canadian employment spells to be clustered around 10-12 weeks and 20 weeks, the former being (during the period analysed) the UI qualification requirement in high unemployment regions for regular claimants and the latter being the entrance requirement for new entrants and re-entrants. These features of the UI program, which were introduced in the late 1970s, appear to have played a role in the emergence of the Canada-US unemployment differential during the 1980s.[4] Other recent research has also found "spikes" in the distribution of employment durations at these points.[5]

Further evidence comes from the analysis of behaviour during 1990 when, due to a political standoff unrelated to the UI program, the variable entrance requirement was suspended [see Baker and Rea (1993) and Green and Riddell (1993b)]. As a consequence, the minimum qualifying period changed from 10 to 14 weeks (depending on the regional unemployment rate) to a flat 14 weeks throughout Canada. In the maximum entitlement regions[6] the entrance requirement increased from 10 to 14 weeks. Analysis of data for 1989 (prior to the suspension of the variable entrance requirement) and 1990 show a spike in the distribution of employment durations (or in the exit or hazard rate out of employment) at 10 weeks in 1989; this spike disappears in 1990 and the one at 14 weeks increases substantially. It appears that many of the jobs which ended at 10 weeks in 1989 were extended to 14 or more weeks in 1990.

Furthermore, when the data set is split into two groups – jobs ending because of a quit and jobs ending because of a layoff – the observed behavioral response is almost entirely due to layoffs. This suggests that employers also respond to the change in the entrance requirement, with the UI program features in place since the late 1970s perhaps encouraging, at least for some individuals in some provinces, a pattern of short periods of employment followed by long periods of UI receipt. Indeed, under the UI provisions introduced in 1978 and in place for much of the subsequent period, 10 weeks of employment in a high unemployment region entitled the individual to 42 weeks of benefits, a pattern which could be repeated annually.[7]

Finally, recent research by Corak (1993), using longitudinal administrative data covering the period 1971-1989, indicates that there is a substantial amount of repeat use of UI in Canada. Individuals with a history of UI participation and short employment spells are much more likely than other individuals to experience another claim in the future. Repetition over a short horizon (defined as within 14 weeks of the end of a previous claim) is closely related to seasonal employment, while repetition over longer periods (within five years of the end of a previous claim) is related to regional and industrial patterns of labour turnover.

Implications of high and rising payroll taxes

As discussed in the main text, payroll taxes play an important role in the labour market since they directly influence the rate of return from decisions to enter employment and increase hours worked, to undertake training, and to bargain for a higher gross wage. These effects are perhaps best analysed using the overall "tax wedge", that is, the difference between the cost of employing someone and the consumption which can eventually be financed from this work (see Table 14 in the main text). With regards to Canada, the tax wedge has gone from being significantly below the OECD average in 1978 to around the OECD average. More importantly Canada has experienced the largest increase of all countries displayed (especially since 1989), as well as remaining significantly above the non-European OECD countries.

Diagram A3 plots the unemployment rate against the overall tax wedge (shown in Table 14 of the main text) across several countries. Although this does not indicate a significant positive relationship, there is a strong negative correlation between the share of wages in business sector value added and the social security contribution rate of employers (see OECD, 1994, Chapter 8). This could result both from wages declining as employers' contributions rise, or from the total amount of labour employed falling.

Recent OECD evidence illustrates the relationship between rising tax rates and unemployment (OECD, 1994, Chapter 8) Table A2 provides estimates of the effects of a rise in various marginal and average tax rates on labour costs in 10 OECD countries, including Canada. The value 1.0 in the first column indicates that when an employers' social security contributions are increased by 1 per cent, labour costs rise by the same amount. That is, high coefficients indicate high wage resistance, with workers succeeding

Diagram A3. **OVERALL TAX WEDGE AND LEVEL OF UNEMPLOYMENT**

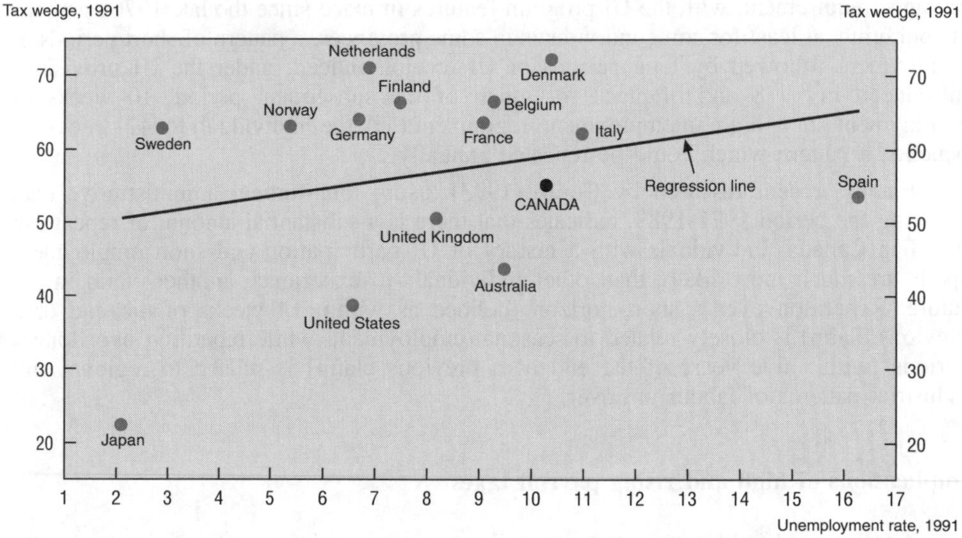

Source: OECD (1994).

142

Table A.2. **Labour cost responses to changes in tax rates**

	Elasticity of labour cost with respect to:		
	Employers' social security contributions	Value added taxes and Exercices	Income taxes and employees' social security contributions
Germany	1.0	1.0	1.0
Canada	**1.0**	**1.0**	**1.0**
Japan	0.5	0.5	0.5
Finland	0.5	0.5	0.5
Australia	0.5	0.5	0.5
France	0.4	0.4	0.4
Italy	0.4	0.4	0.4
Sweden	0.0	1.0	0.0
United States	0.0	0.0	1.0
United Kingdom	0.25	0.25	0.25

Note: Since in some countries the effect of income tax systems contains impacts of both average and marginal tax rates, the elasticities in this table have been calculated on the assumption that these two rates move conjointly. This assumption is important as far as Japan, Canada, Finland and Italy are concerned. Estimates cover the private businnes sector and the estimation method is the FIML-procedure proposed by Johansen (1991) for estimation of long-run relationships in multivariate systems.
Source: OECD (1994).

in protecting their disposable incomes in response to a tax rise. The degree of responsiveness differs significantly across the countries considered, with Canada proving to be a relatively rigid wage economy in the face of increased taxes.

These results have been used to assess the impact of changes in taxation on unemployment, by linking labour costs to employment and unemployment. Diagram A4 illustrates simulation results for three types of countries; high wage resistance (Canada), medium wage resistance (France), and low wage resistance (United States). In each case a tax increase of 1 percentage point is simulated, leading to an immediate rise in labour costs by 1 percentage point. However, only in Canada does the labour cost increase persist, leading to both a persistent decline in employment and a rise in unemployment. That is, the rise in labour costs induced by tax increases did not lead to a fall in real wages, resulting in increased unemployment. These results suggest that, by shifting the incidence of average and marginal tax rates, beneficial labour market impacts are possible. This might include reducing the tax burden on particular sectors or activities which are particularly labour intensive, or on low income individuals.

Diagram A4. SIMULATED IMPACT OF A RISE IN EMPLOYERS' SOCIAL SECURITY CONTRIBUTIONS[1]

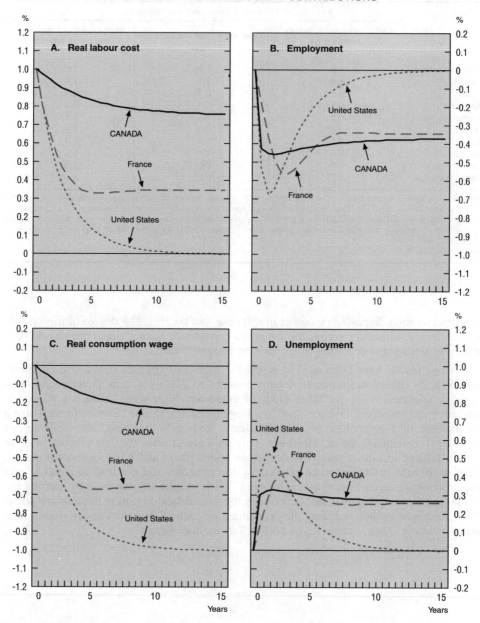

1. The simulated effect of a rise by one percentage point in employers' social security contribution rate.
Source: OECD (1994).

Notes

1. For example, both France (1987) and New Zealand (1990) raised the requirements of the long-term unemployed to attend interviews, with 5 and 8 per cent respectively of those called immediately struck off the list due to their non-attendance.

2. A similar incentive structure could be achieved by enforcing severance pay obligations in cases that lead to justified UI claims (*i.e.* claims not following a voluntary quit).

3. For recent surveys of this work see Corak (1994), Green and Riddell (1993) and Phipps (1993).

4. Card and Riddell (1993, p. 185) conclude that: ''Relative increases in the number of Canadian men and women reporting exactly 10 or 12 weeks of employment, and relative increases in the weeks of unemployment reported by these workers, account for 13 per cent of the relative rise in female unemployment and 22 per cent of the relative rise in male unemployment. Similar increases for women with exactly 20 weeks of work account for another 8 per cent of the relative rise in female unemployment. UI recipiency rates also increased for Canadian men and women with these labour supply patterns. These findings point to a significant role of the UI system in accounting for the rise in relative Canadian unemployment, although most of the rise in the Canadian-US unemployment gap remains unexplained.''

5. See Christofides and McKenna (1993), Baker and Rea (1993) and Green and Riddell (1993*b*).

6. Unemployment regions, of which there are 62, are generally smaller than provinces.

7. In fact, given that there is a 2 week waiting period in which no benefits are paid, a pattern of 10 weeks employment and 40 weeks of benefits could be repeated annually in those regions. As noted in the text, under the current regulations 12 weeks of work are required, and these would entitle the claimant to 32 weeks of benefits in a maximum entitlement region.

Annex II

Chronology of economic events

1993

January

The chartered banks' prime lending rate falls to 7 per cent.

February

Canadian National Railways outlines plans to eliminate 11 000 of its 32 000 jobs.

March

The Saskatchewan government's 1993/94 budget halves the deficit by ways of sales tax increases and cuts in agricultural support and spending on education and health.

The banks' prime lending rate drops to a 20-year low of 6 per cent.

April

The federal government presents its 1993/94 budget calling for a fall in the deficit to C$ 32.6 billion from an estimated outcome of C$ 35.5 billion in 1992/93. The budget incorporates the measures announced in the December Economic and Fiscal Statement. Total spending is expected to rise by less than 1 per cent in 1993/94, and plans to cut 16 500 jobs in the federal public service are announced.

The Manitoba budget extends the range of items covered by the provincial sales tax and calls for a decline in overall spending in 1993/94.

The province of New Brunswick's 1993 budget increases income taxes, broadens the coverage of the provincial sales tax, and reduces grants to university students, seniors and municipalities.

The British Columbia budget for 1993/94 raises indirect taxes while maintaining high expenditure growth.

The Ontario government announces a C$ 2.4 billion spending reduction programme, including the elimination of around 10 000 jobs and closure of many government agencies.

May

The Ontario government releases its 1993/94 budget. With a fall in overall spending and higher personal, corporate and sales taxes, the deficit is expected to decline to just over C$ 9 billion from almost C$ 12 billion in 1992/93.

The government of Quebec intends to limit the budget deficit in 1993/94 to just over C$ 4 billion by raising income taxes and keeping expenditure growth at under 1 per cent.

The Alberta government announces a marked reduction in overall spending in the 1993/94 fiscal year.

July

Banks lower their prime lending rate to a 26-year low of 5¾ per cent.

August

The Ontario government's social contract comes into effect, cutting almost C$ 2 billion from the wages and benefits of public sector workers.

The federal government announces the closure of most of the cod fishery in Newfoundland due to record low fish stocks. About 12 000 people are affected, in addition to the 30 000 workers left jobless by the ban on cod fishing since 1992.

October

A Liberal majority federal government is elected on 25 October, replacing the Progressive Conservative Party in power since 1984.

The new Nova Scotia government introduces its 1993/94 budget providing for indirect tax increases and significant expenditure cuts.

November

The banks' prime lending rate falls to 5 per cent, a 31-year low.

December

The Ontario government introduces the first minimum corporate tax in Canada, to be phased in over three years.

The federal government closes all but one Atlantic Canada cod fishery and curtails catches of other species, resulting in a further loss of 500 jobs.

1994

January

The governments of Ontario and Quebec sign an agreement committing them to remove trade barriers in construction contracting and labour mobility.

The Bank of Canada's discount rate falls to below 4 per cent, the lowest level in 30 years.

February

The federal government tables its 1994/95 budget calling for a decline in the deficit to C\$ 39.7 billion from an estimated outcome of C\$ 45.7 billion in 1993/94. Specific measures include the closure of military bases and military spending cuts over five years; the freeze of public service wages for another two years; the tightening of eligibility requirements for unemployment benefits; the elimination of capital gains exemptions; and cuts in the business entertainment tax deduction.

The Alberta government budget calls for spending cuts of the order of C\$ 1 billion – including the areas of health, welfare and education – to bring the deficit down to C\$ 1½ billion in 1994/95.

The federal, Quebec, New Brunswick and Ontario governments slash cigarette taxes in an effort to reduce smuggling.

March

The commercial banks raise their prime lending rate to 6¼ per cent.

The Newfoundland budget calls for a sharp reduction in the deficit in 1994/95, and a balanced budget by 1995/96.

April

Banks increase their prime lending rate to 6¾ per cent.

The Manitoba budget calls for a gradual fall in the deficit, with limited spending cuts and higher gambling revenues.

The British Columbia government imposes a C\$ 2 billion tax on forestry companies to finance a provincial job creation programme.

The federal government announces a C\$ 2 billion five-year aid programme for Atlantic fishermen and plant workers, covering about 30 000 people.

May

The Quebec budget calls for a slight decline in the deficit to C\$ 4½ billion in 1994/95, combining modest spending cuts with tax breaks and new fiscal incentives.

The Ontario budget aims at lowering the deficit from C\$ 9¹/₂ billion in 1993/94 to C\$ 8¹/₂ billion in 1994/95, with limited spending cuts and tax reductions.

June

Banks raise their prime lending rate to 8 per cent.

July

The federal and provincial governments signed an agreement to ease internal trade barriers from July 1995.

Banks reduce their prime lending rate in two steps to 7¹/₂ per cent.

August

The trade dispute between Canada and the United States over softwood lumber exports was settled in Canada's favour by an extraordinary challenge committee under the terms of the Free Trade Agreement. The US government is expected to refund countervailing duties collected from Canadian companies since 1992.

Banks reduce their prime lending rate to 7¹/₄ per cent.

September

Banks reduce their prime lending rate to 7 per cent.

STATISTICAL ANNEX

Selected background statistics

	Moyenne 1984-93	1984	1985	1986	1987	1988	1989	1990	1991	1992	1993
A. Percentage changes											
Private consumption[1]	2.9	4.6	5.2	4.4	4.4	4.5	3.4	1.0	-1.5	1.3	1.6
Gross fixed capital formation[1]	3.5	2.1	9.5	6.2	10.8	10.3	6.1	-3.5	-2.2	-2.8	-0.2
Public investment[1]	4.5	6.5	11.1	-1.6	2.2	3.6	8.8	6.9	4.7	-0.6	4.4
Private investment[1]	3.3	1.5	9.2	7.4	12.0	11.1	5.7	-4.8	-3.1	-3.2	-0.9
Residential[1]	2.5	0.5	9.8	13.3	16.4	2.8	4.8	-9.7	-12.5	7.9	-4.4
Non-residential[1]	3.6	1.7	8.7	4.2	9.7	15.8	6.2	-2.4	1.1	-7.5	0.7
GDP[1]	2.6	6.3	4.8	3.3	4.2	5.0	2.4	-0.2	-1.8	0.6	2.2
GDP price deflator	3.1	3.1	2.6	2.4	4.7	4.6	4.8	3.1	2.7	1.4	1.1
Industrial production	2.4	12.2	5.6	-0.8	4.9	5.3	-0.1	-3.3	-4.1	0.9	4.9
Employment	1.5	2.4	2.6	2.8	2.9	3.2	2.0	0.7	-1.8	-0.8	1.2
Compensation of employees (current prices)	6.1	7.7	7.8	6.7	8.7	9.7	7.9	5.2	2.6	2.4	2.5
Productivity (real GDP/employment)	1.1	3.8	2.1	0.5	1.3	1.7	0.5	-0.9	0	1.4	1.0
Unit labour costs (compensation/real GDP)	3.4	1.3	2.9	3.3	4.4	4.5	5.3	5.5	4.5	1.8	0.3
B. Percentage ratios											
Gross fixed capital formation as per cent of GDP at constant prices	21.3	18.7	19.5	20.1	21.4	22.4	23.2	22.5	22.4	21.6	21.1
Stockbuilding as per cent of GDP at constant prices	0.2	0.7	0.4	0.5	0.6	0.5	0.7	-0.3	-0.5	-0.6	0.2
Foreign balance as per cent of GDP at constant prices	-0.8	2.3	1.7	0.9	0.1	-1.1	-2.6	-2.1	-2.8	-2.4	-2.0
Compensation of employees as per cent of GDP at current prices	55.0	53.7	53.9	54.3	54.2	54.1	54.3	55.6	56.6	56.8	56.3
Direct taxes as per cent of household income	15.6	13.5	13.7	14.8	15.4	15.8	15.6	17.3	17.0	16.5	16.1
Household saving as per cent of disposable income	10.7	15.0	13.3	10.7	9.2	9.7	10.4	9.7	9.6	9.8	9.2
Unemployment rate	9.6	11.2	10.5	9.5	8.8	7.8	7.5	8.1	10.3	11.3	11.2
C. Other indicator											
Current balance (billion dollars)	-15.8	-0.6	-4.5	-10.1	-11.8	-17.1	-22.8	-21.6	-24.1	-21.9	-23.8

1. At constant 1986 prices.

153

Table A. **Supply and use of resources**

Million canadian dollars, current prices

	1984	1985	1986	1987	1988	1989	1990	1991	1992	1993
Private consumption	251 645	274 503	297 478	322 769	349 937	378 933	399 319	412 246	423 055	437 289
Public consumption	89 089	95 519	100 129	105 836	114 472	124 108	135 157	144 436	149 731	153 121
Gross fixed investment	84 699	94 198	101 560	116 717	132 790	146 075	141 376	132 688	128 155	126 942
Final domestic demand	425 433	464 220	499 167	545 322	597 199	649 116	675 852	689 370	700 941	717 352
	(7.1)	(9.1)	(7.5)	(9.2)	(9.5)	(8.7)	(4.1)	(2.0)	(1.7)	(2.3)
Stockbuilding	4 761	2 281	2 557	3 071	3 795	3 607	–2 835	–3 675	–3 280	1 263
	(1.9)	(–0.6)	(0.1)	(0.1)	(0.1)	(0)	(–1.0)	(–0.1)	(0.1)	(0.7)
Total domestic demand	430 194	466 501	501 724	548 393	600 994	652 723	673 017	685 695	697 661	718 615
	(9.1)	(8.4)	(7.6)	(9.3)	(9.6)	(8.6)	(3.1)	(1.9)	(1.7)	(3.0)
Exports	126 035	134 919	138 119	145 416	159 309	163 903	168 917	163 943	180 406	208 223
Imports	110 632	123 388	133 369	140 502	156 384	166 079	171 223	172 453	186 738	212 508
Foreign balance	15 403	11 531	4 750	4 914	2 925	–2 176	–2 306	–8 510	–6 332	–4 285
	(0.4)	(–0.9)	(–1.4)	(0)	(–0.4)	(–0.8)	(0)	(–0.9)	(–0.3)	(0.3)
Statistical discrepancy	–862	–44	–808	–1 710	1 987	201	–1 244	–2 419	–2 938	–2 672
GDP (market prices)	444 735	477 988	505 666	551 597	605 906	650 748	669 467	674 766	688 391	711 658
	(9.6)	(7.5)	(5.8)	(9.1)	(9.8)	(7.4)	(2.9)	(0.8)	(2.0)	(3.4)

Note: Figures in parentheses are annual growth rates; for stockbuilding and the foreign balance they are contributions to GDP growth.
Source: CANSIM – Statistics Canada.

154

Table A. **Supply and use of resources** *(cont'd)*

Million canadian dollars, 1986 prices

	1984	1985	1986	1987	1988	1989	1990	1991	1992	1993
Private consumption	270 854	284 923	297 478	310 453	324 301	335 284	338 717	333 753	338 198	343 666
Public consumption	95 571	98 585	100 129	101 857	106 060	110 331	113 890	117 063	118 457	119 107
Gross fixed investment	87 362	95 624	101 560	112 542	124 105	131 630	126 962	124 187	120 680	120 441
Final domestic demand	453 787	479 132	499 167	524 852	554 466	577 245	579 569	575 003	577 335	583 214
	(3.4)	(5.6)	(4.2)	(5.1)	(5.6)	(4.1)	(0.4)	(−0.8)	(0.4)	(1.0)
Stockbuilding	3 423	2 177	2 557	3 222	2 515	3 778	−1 737	−2 906	−3 469	985
	(1.3)	(−0.3)	(0.1)	(0.1)	(−0.1)	(0.2)	(−1.0)	(−0.2)	(−0.1)	(0.8)
Total domestic demand	457 210	481 309	501 724	528 074	556 981	581 023	577 832	572 097	573 866	584 199
	(4.7)	(5.3)	(4.2)	(5.3)	(5.5)	(4.3)	(−0.5)	(−1.0)	(0.3)	(1.8)
Exports	124 785	132 218	138 119	142 942	156 528	157 799	164 312	165 984	178 797	197 436
Imports	114 058	123 935	133 369	142 678	162 385	172 584	175 960	181 359	192 127	208 958
Foreign balance	10 727	8 283	4 750	264	−5 857	−14 785	−11 648	−15 375	−13 330	−11 522
	(0.5)	(−0.5)	(−0.7)	(−0.9)	(−1.2)	(−1.6)	(0.6)	(−0.7)	(0.4)	(0.3)
Statistical discrepancy	−770	−155	−808	−1 608	1 834	248	−1 029	−1 987	−2 371	−2 136
GDP (market prices)	467 167	489 437	505 666	526 730	552 958	566 486	565 155	554 735	558 165	570 541
	(6.3)	(4.8)	(3.3)	(4.2)	(5.0)	(2.4)	(−0.2)	(−1.8)	(0.6)	(2.2)

Note: Figures in parentheses are annual growth rates; for stockbuilding and the foreign balance they are contributions to GDP growth.
Source: CANSIM – Statistics Canada.

Table B. Industrial production, employment and other business indicators

Seasonally adjusted

	1989	1990	1991	1992	1993	1993 II	1993 III	1993 IV	1994 I	1994 II
Indices of industrial production (1985 = 100)										
Total	109.4	105.8	101.5	102.4	107.4	106.9	107.8	108.9	109.6	112.8
Durable manufactures	117.0	110.5	101.6	103.0	110.6	108.9	110.6	114.1	114.3	118.1
Non-durable manufactures	106.5	104.9	99.1	99.1	101.3	101.5	101.2	101.4	102.0	104.2
New Residential construction (thousands, annual rates)										
Starts	215.4	181.6	156.2	168.3	155.4	187.3	179.8	160.8	95.5	205.5
Completions[1]	217.4	206.2	160.0	173.2	161.8	146.4	210.3	165.4	115.1	148.6
Under construction[2]	127.6	100.7	95.0	87.5	79.8	89.5	81.9	79.8	74.7	89.1
Employment and unemployment, (thousands, monthly averages)										
Civilian labour force	13 502	13 681	13 755	13 796	13 946	13 948	13 977	13 989	14 023	14 077
Non-agricultural employment	12 056	12 141	11 890	11 807	11 934	11 906	11 948	11 998	12 062	12 171
Employment[3]										
Mining	155	152	145	129	120	120	120	120	122	..
Manufacturing	2 004	1 885	1 692	1 599	1 597	1 603	1 637	1 594	1 558	1 648
Durables	1 088	1 005	885	851	839	839	858	838	831	..
Non-durables	916	880	806	748	758	764	779	755	727	..
Transportation, communication and other utilities[4]	886	902	860	852	841	849	848	833	820	..
Unemployment (thousands)	1 018	1 110	1 416	1 556	1 562	1 582	1 581	1 552	1 544	1 503
Unemployment (percentage of civilian labour force)	7.5	8.1	10.3	11.3	11.2	11.4	11.3	11.1	11.0	10.7
Average weekly hours worked in manufacturing	38.6	38.2	37.9	38.3	38.6	38.7	38.6	38.6	38.8	38.9
Retail sales ($ million, monthly averages)	15 775	16 047	15 101	15 421	16 154	16 044	16 254	16 419	16 959	17 172

Table B. **Industrial production, employment and other business indicators** *(cont'd)*

Seasonally adjusted

	1989	1990	1991	1992	1993	1993 II	1993 III	1993 IV	1994 I	1994 II
Orders and inventories in manufacturing ($ million)										
New orders (monthly averages)[5]	25 716	24 641	23 313	23 924	26 132	25 402	25 782	27 063	27 098	28 630
Unfilled orders (end of period)	29 635	26 052	25 247	25 959	29 646	28 412	28 050	29 646	30 535	31 159
Total inventories (end of period)	44 523	45 118	42 319	42 181	43 572	42 575	43 035	43 572	44 681	45 447

1. Not seasonally adjusted.
2. Not seasonally adjusted, end of period.
3. Estimates of employment, earnings and hours from april 1983 are based on a revised survey and are not seasonally adjusted.
4. Includes storage, electric power gas and water utilities.
5. 3-month averages for quarters.
Source: OECD, *Main Economic Indicators*; CANSIM – Statistics Canada.

Table C. **Prices, wages and finance**

	1989	1990	1991	1992	1993	1993 II	1993 III	1993 IV	1994 I	1994 II
Prices (1985 = 100)										
Consumer prices all items	118.7	124.4	131.4	133.4	135.8	135.4	136.0	136.7	136.0	135.5
of which:										
Food	116.7	121.5	127.3	126.8	128.9	129.1	129.0	129.0	129.4	129.3
Non-food	119.3	125.1	132.4	134.9	137.4	136.9	137.6	138.5	137.6	137.0
Producer prices manufactured goods	110.4	110.7	109.5	110.1	113.7	113.0	113.7	115.0	116.9	118.9
Wages and profits										
Hourly earnings in manufacturing (1985 = 100)	116.4	121.9	127.6	132.1	134.8	134.7	134.1	135.1	137.6	137.3
Corporate profits before tax ($ million, annual rates)	60 093	44 814	33 706	33 053	39 769	40 208	40 496	42 444	49 392	52 356
Banking ($ million, end of period)										
Chartered banks:										
Canadian dollar deposits	274 630	297 995	311 952	339 085	377 231	354 942	373 243	377 231	376 430	393 667
of which:										
Personal savings deposits	184 228	202 597	216 515	228 732	263 766	248 134	262 507	263 766	261 421	273 169
Liquid assets	28 084	32 099	46 535	57 865	82 181	69 218	75 437	82 181	76 299	78 446
Holdings of Govt. of Canada direct and guaranteed securities	3 451	6 488	11 819	17 388	32 829	26 731	31 704	32 829	35 557	34 421
Total loans	280 458	290 814	305 814	323 996	357 878	330 737	346 466	357 878	367 438	382 454
Currency outside banks	18 437	19 099	20 373	22 000	23 603	22 992	23 388	23 603	24 413	24 791
Interest rates (per cent, end of period)										
Prime corporate paper (3 month)	12.4	11.7	7.6	7.3	4.0	4.6	4.8	4.0	5.8	6.6
Yield of long-term Govt. bonds	9.7	10.4	9.1	8.6	7.3	8.1	7.4	7.3	7.8	9.1
Miscellaneous										
Share prices Toronto stock exchange (1985 = 100)	140.1	126.1	127.9	125.5	143.9	143.0	148.6	156.8	163.5	155.1

Source: OECD, *Main Economic Indicators;* CANSIM – Statistics Canada.

Table D. **Balance of payments**

Million US dollars

	1989	1990	1991	1992	1993	1993 II	1993 III	1993 IV	1994 I	1994 II
Current account										
Merchandise exports	88 685	89 646	89 024	98 007	115 294	122 963	128 411	125 941	132 413	144 045
Merchandise imports	72 654	77 074	81 344	89 047	107 204	116 989	120 113	122 247	126 355	136 429
Trade balance	16 032	12 573	7 680	8 959	8 090	5 974	8 298	3 694	6 058	7 616
Services, net	-16 483	-16 892	-17 978	-20 699	-25 475	-28 969	-29 847	-27 756	-28 061	-31 607
Travel	-1 642	-1 541	-839	-1 907	-2 387	-3 631	-5 792	-6 599	-6 747	-6 106
Investment income	-12 346	-12 761	-13 718	-15 446	-19 759	-21 157	-19 574	-16 636	-16 764	-20 669
Other services	-2 495	-2 590	-3 421	-3 346	-3 329	-4 181	-4 481	-4 521	-4 550	-4 832
Transfers, net	-176	-215	187	-53	241	236	-63	13	97	191
Private	178	174	238	602	878	966	955	912	858	837
Official	-354	-389	-51	-655	-637	-730	-1 018	-899	-761	-646
Current balance	-627	-4 534	-10 111	-11 793	-17 144	-22 759	-21 612	-24 048	-21 907	-23 800
Capital account										
Long-term capital, net	4 025	5 072	15 222	8 270	10 448	14 244	10 454	10 870	7 972	19 245
Private direct	1 069	-2 564	-720	-500	2 608	435	3 120	-2 943	888	-1 246
Private portfolio	4 467	8 272	15 960	9 220	8 285	14 637	8 568	15 370	8 487	20 500
Public[1]	-1 510	-635	-18	-450	-445	-829	-1 233	-1 557	-1 402	-9
Short-term capital, net	-432	3 124	-3 667	7 714	14 851	8 276	13 122	12 995	6 920	9 273
Private non monetary	-981	2 471	-1 915	3 242	6 705	8 279	8 017	7 171	9 281	1 232
Private monetary institutions	-736	999	-3 284	3 385	2 295	-484	2 197	3 782	-4 014	-497
Official non-monetary	1 285	-346	1 532	1 087	5 851	481	2 908	2 042	1 653	8 538
Miscellaneous official accounts	960	870	972	1 547	-6	-2	-3	-4	-3	3
Allocation of SDRs	0	0	0	0	0	0	0	0	0	0
Errors and omissions	-4 770	-4 613	-1 936	-2 372	-475	533	-1 405	-2 281	1 237	-5 185
Change in reserves	-843	-81	476	3 363	7 674	291	556	-2 469	-5 780	-464

1. Excludes special transactions.
Source: Statistics Canada; OECD Secretariat.

Table E. **Public sector**

A. BUDGET INDICATORS: GENERAL GOVERNMENT ACCOUNTS
(per cent of GDP)[1]

	1960	1970	1980	1992	1993
Current receipts	26.0	34.3	36.1	43.1	42.6
Non-interest expenditure	26.1	31.2	34.9	42.3	42.0
Primary budget balance	–0.6	1.9	–0.9	–2.3	–2.4
Net interest payments	1.1	1.1	1.9	4.8	4.7
General government budget balance	–1.7	0.8	–2.8	–7.1	–7.1
of which:					
Federal	–0.6	0.3	–3.4	–4.2	–4.6
Provincial, local, hospitals	–1.1	–0.8	–0.3	–2.9	–2.3
Pension plans[2]	0.0	1.3	1.0	0.0	–0.1
General government debt					
Gross debt	66.9*	52.9	44.6	87.5	92.2
Net debt	26.7*	11.7	13.5	57.1	61.8
of which:					
Federal	18.9*	7.3	16.2	50.0	52.0

B. THE STRUCTURE OF EXPENDITURE
(per cent of GDP)

	1960	1970	1980	1992	1993
Total general government expenditure	28.8	34.9	40.3	51.5	51.1
Current consumption	13.4	18.5	19.1	21.8	21.5
Transfers to persons	7.8	7.8	9.8	15.6	16.0
Subsidies (+ capital assistance)	0.8	1.1	3.0	2.2	1.8
Capital formation	3.8	3.5	2.7	2.3	2.3
Other programme expenditure	0.2	0.3	0.3	0.4	0.4
Total programme expenditure	26.0	31.2	34.9	42.3	42.0
Gross interest payments	2.8	3.6	5.4	9.2	9.1

C. GENERAL GOVERNMENT EXPENDITURE BY FUNCTION, FINANCIAL MANAGEMENT SYSTEM BASIS
(per cent of GDP, fiscal year)

	1965-66	1970-71	1980-81	1990-91	1991-92
Social services	5.4	6.7	8.6	10.2	11.6
Education	5.2	6.8	5.8	5.6	6.0
Health	2.9	4.8	5.2	6.3	6.8
Transport and Communication	3.7	3.1	3.0	2.3	2.3
National Defence	2.7	2.0	1.6	1.7	1.6
General Services	1.7	2.6	2.8	2.7	2.8

* 1961.
1. National accounts basis.
2. Canada and Quebec Pension Plans.
Source: Department of Finance.

Table F. **Financial markets**

	1970	1980	1992	1993
SIZE OF THE FINANCIAL SECTOR (percentages) [1]				
Sector employment/total employment	4.8	5.7	6.2	6.2
Net financial assets/GDP	6.3	4.3	6.2	6.9
STRUCTURE OF FINANCIAL ASSETS AND LIABILITIES				
Financial institutions' share in domestic financial assets (per cent)	34.0	38.6	41.0	41.5
Government securities in NFB [2] total financial assets (per cent)	0.3	0.1	2.7	2.3
STRUCTURE OF NFB LIABILITIES				
Debt to equity ratio [3]	1.17	1.42	1.46	1.48
Short-term:				
Securities and mortgages ($ billion)	8.7	33.4	109.4	119.8
Trade payables ($ billion)	12.4	54.9	94.9	96.5
Long-term:				
Bonds ($ billion)	13.7	28.7	89.3	97.7
Loans and corporate claims ($ billion)	27.0	105.5	250.6	256.6
INTERNATIONALISATION OF MARKETS				
Share of foreign currency assets and liabilities in the banking sector [4]				
Assets	28.9	39.1	32.9	30.8
Liabilities	28.6	40.2	35.1	33.3
Foreign purchases of Canadian securities [5]	12.4	18.2	60.3	75.4
Canadian purchases of foreign securities [5]	−1.2	0.6	18.8	20.0
DEBT (per cent of GDP)				
Private non-financial sector				
NFB [2, 6]	77.3	81.6	85.9	88.0
Households [7]	45.3	52.5	62.8	64.0

1. Public and private financial institutions and insurance.
2. NFB = non-financial corporate business, excluding farms.
3. (Liabilities − shares)/shares.
4. Per cent of consolidated balance sheet of chartered banks, exludes other deposit-taking institutions.
5. Per cent of net issues on domestic securities markets. Data include new issues as well as secondary market transactions.
6. Liabilities less shares.
7. Persons and unincorporated business liabilities less trade payables, other loans and other Canadian bonds.
Source: Bank of Canada Review; Labour Force Survey; National Authorities (National Balance Sheet; Security transactions with non-residents).

Table G. **Labour-market indicators**

A. LABOUR MARKET PERFORMANCE

	Cyclical peak: 1979	Cyclical trough: 1982	1985	1993
Standardised unemployment rate	7.4	10.9	10.4	11.3
Unemployment rate: Total	7.4	11.0	10.5	11.2
Male	6.6	11.0	10.3	11.7
Women	8.8	10.9	10.7	10.6
Youth[1]	12.9	18.7	16.4	17.7
Share of long-term unemployment in total unemployment[2]	3.4	5.4	10.3	13.8
Dispersion of regional unemployment rates[3]	3.4	3.0	3.8	4.0

B. STRUCTURAL OR INSTITUTIONAL CHARACTERISTICS

	1970	1980	1985	1993*
Participation rate:[4] Total	62.4	71.4	73.6	74.9
Male	84.5	85.8	84.6	82.3
Women	40.4	57.2	62.8	67.6
Employment/population (15-64 years)	66.0	65.8	70.2	66.5
Average hours worked	36.0	35.1	34.8	34.4
Part-time work (as per cent of dependent employment)	n.a.	13.0	15.5	17.3
Non-wage labour costs[5] (as percentage of total compensation)	6.1	8.5	9.8	11.8
Government unemployment insurance replacement ratio[6]	22.5	31.2	33.8	36.5
Unionisation rate[7]	36.4	37.6	39.0	37.4

Average percentage changes (annual rates)	1970/1960	1980/1970	1993*/1980
Labour force	2.7	3.3	1.4
Employment: Total	2.9	3.1	1.1
Goods-producing	0.6	1.8	–0.7
Services	4.3	4.1	1.9

*   Or latest available year.
1.   People between 15 and 24 years as a percentage of the labour force of the same age group.
2.   People looking for a job since one year or more.
3.   Measured by standard deviation for 10 provinces.
4.   Labour force as a percentage of relevant population group, aged between 15 and 64 years.
5.   Employers' contributions to social security and pension funds.
6.   Unemployment benefits per unemployed divided by the compensation per employee.
7.   Figures for 1970 are 1970-79 average.
Source: CANSIM – Statistics Canada; Canadian Authorities; OECD Secretariat.

Table H. Production structure and performance indicators

A. PRODUCTION STRUCTURE	Per cent share of GDP at factor cost (constant prices)			Per cent share of total employment		
	1975	1980	1993	1975	1980	1993
Agriculture	2.8	2.4	2.3	5.2	4.5	3.6
Mining and quarrying	5.4	4.5	4.2	1.5	1.8	1.2
Manufacturing	20.4	19.7	17.8	20.2	19.7	14.5
of which:						
Food	2.3	2.3	1.8	2.5	2.4	1.9
Paper and paper products	1.8	2.0	1.5	1.4	1.3	1.0
Primary metal industries	1.9	1.4	1.5	1.3	1.3	0.8
Fabricated metal products, machinery and equipment	4.7	4.7	4.8	4.6		
Chemicals and chemical products	1.2	1.3	1.5	0.9	1.0	0.8
Construction	6.4	6.4	5.3	6.5	5.8	5.3
Market services	57.7	59.2	63.0	58.7	60.2	67.6
of which:						
Transport, storage and communication	7.4	7.8	8.5	7.6	7.3	6.2
Wholesale and retail trade	11.3	10.7	12.1	17.6	17.2	17.3
Finance, insurance and real estate	13.6	14.9	16.9	5.1	5.7	6.2
Community, business social and personal services	22.3	22.4	22.3	27.2	28.9	36.8
Government services	8.1	7.4	6.5	7.2	6.9	6.9

B. MANUFACTURING SECTOR PERFORMANCE (constant prices)	Productivity growth by sector (GDP/employment, annual rate)		
	$\frac{1980}{1975}$	$\frac{1990}{1980}$	$\frac{1993}{1980}$
Manufacturing	0.4	2.7	2.8
of which:			
Food	1.4	1.8	1.4
Paper and paper products	3.6	0.9	1.4
Primary metal industries	−5.4	2.8	5.3
Chemicals and chemical products	1.3	4.6	3.9

Source: Canadian authorities; OECD, *National Accounts.*

163

BASIC STATISTICS:

INTERNATIONAL COMPARISONS

	Units	Reference period [1]	Australia	Austria
Population				
Total	Thousands	1991	17 292	7 823
Inhabitants per sq. km	Number	1991	2	93
Net average annual increase over previous 10 years	%	1991	1.5	0.3
Employment				
Total civilian employment (TCE) [2]	Thousands	1991	7 705	3 482
Of which: Agriculture	% of TCE		5.5	7.4
Industry	% of TCE		24.2	36.9
Services	% of TCE		70.4	55.8
Gross domestic product (GDP)				
At current prices and current exchange rates	Bill. US$	1991	297.4	164.7
Per capita	US$		17 200	21 048
At current prices using current PPP's [3]	Bill. US$	1991	280	135.6
Per capita	US$		16 195	17 329
Average annual volume growth over previous 5 years	%	1991	2.8	3.3
Gross fixed capital formation (GFCF)	% of GDP	1991	20.5	25.1
Of which: Machinery and equipment	% of GDP		8.8	10.4
Residential construction	% of GDP		4.6	4.6 (9)
Average annual volume growth over previous 5 years	%	1991	0.3	5.2
Gross saving ratio [4]	% of GDP	1991	17.2	25.6
General government				
Current expenditure on goods and services	% of GDP	1991	18.3	18.2
Current disbursements [5]	% of GDP	1991	36.6	45.7
Current receipts	% of GDP	1991	33.7	47.2
Net official development assistance	% of GDP	1991	0.35	0.33
Indicators of living standards				
Private consumption per capita using current PPP's [3]	US$	1991	9 827	9 591
Passenger cars, per 1 000 inhabitants	Number	1990	430	382
Telephones, per 1 000 inhabitants	Number	1990	448 (89)	589
Television sets, per 1 000 inhabitants	Number	1989	484	475
Doctors, per 1 000 inhabitants	Number	1991	2	2.1
Infant mortality per 1 000 live births	Number	1991	7.1	7.4
Wages and prices (average annual increase over previous 5 years)				
Wages (earnings or rates according to availability)	%	1991	5.4	5.2
Consumer prices	%	1991	6.7	2.5
Foreign trade				
Exports of goods, fob*	Mill. US$	1991	39 764	40 985
As % of GDP	%		13.4	24.9
Average annual increase over previous 5 years	%		13.2	12.8
Imports of goods, cif*	Mill. US$	1991	38 844	48 914
As % of GDP	%		13.1	29.7
Average annual increase over previous 5 years	%		10.1	13.7
Total official reserves [6]	Mill. SDR's	1991	11 432	6 591
As ratio of average monthly imports of goods	Ratio		3.5	1.6

* At current prices and exchange rates.
1. Unless otherwise stated.
2. According to the definitions used in OECD *Labour Force Statistics.*
3. PPP's = Purchasing Power Parities.
4. Gross saving = Gross national disposable income minus private and government consumption.
5. Current disbursements = Current expenditure on goods and services plus current transfers and payments of property income.
6. Gold included in reserves is valued at 35 SDR's per ounce. End of year.
7. Including Luxembourg.

	Belgium	Canada	Denmark	Finland	France	Germany	Greece	Iceland	Ireland
	0 005	27 000	5 154	5 029	57 050	63 889	10 269	258	3 524
	328	3	120	15	104	257	78	3	50
	0.2	1	0.1	0.5	0.5	0.4	0.5	1.1	0.2
	3 735	12 340	2 612	2 330	21 782	28 533	3 768	140	1 113
	2.6	4.5	5.7	8.5	5.8	3.4	22.6	10.7	13.8
	28.1	23.2	27.7	29.2	29.5	39.2	27.5	26.4	28.9
	69.3	72.3	66.6	62.3	64.8	57.4	50	62.9	57.2
	196.9	583.7	130.3	121.2	1 195.8	1 587.8	70.2	6.5	43.4
	9 677	21 617	25 277	24 097	20 961	24 852	6 840	25 232	12 324
	171.5	520.6	90.7	77.8	1 035.6	1 257.8	79.4	4.5	40.5
	7 145	19 281	17 603	15 480	18 152	19 687	7 729	17 442	11 480
	3.2	1.9	1.1	1.4	2.7	3.8	1.9	2	5.4
	19.8	20	16.9	22.4	20.9	21.4	18.6	18.9	17.1
	10.4 (90)	6.4	8.5	7.4	9.4	10	7.8	6	7.7
	4.2	6.2	3.2	6.1	5.1	5.7	4.4	4.1	4.1
	8.5	4.2	−2.9	0.1	4.6	5.4	3.5	2.6	3
	21.4	14.4	17.9	14.7	20.7	23.1	15.3	14.4	23.7
	14.7	21.3	25.1	24.4	18.3	17.7	19.9	20	16.3
	54.6	47.9	57.2	46	47	44.2	47.6	32.5	49.9 (8
	49.8	43.1	55.5	42.6	46.5	44.5	37	35.1	43.7 (8
	0.42	0.45	0.92	0.77	0.62	0.43	0.08	0.12	0.17
	0 756	11 634	9 139	8 686	10 928	10 672	5 516	10 731	6 409
	387	469	311	386	413	480	169	464	228
	546	570	972	530	482	671	458	496	279
	447	626	528	488	400	506	195	319	271
	3.6	2.2	2.8	2.5	2.7	3.2	3.4	2.8	1.5
	8.4	6.8	7.5	5.8	7.3	7.1	9	5.5	8.2
	3.5	4.5	5.9	8.3	3.8	4.7	16.9	. .	5.3
	2.5	4.8	3.7	5.2	3.2	2.1	16.7	17.2	3.2
	8 291 [7]	127 658	34 988	26 508	216 157	409 620	8 014	1 589	23 796
	60.1	21.9	26.9	21.9	18.1	25.8	11.4	24.4	54.8
	11.4	7.9	11.1	7.1	11.7	10.6	8.9	8.1	14
	0 330 [7]	116 729	31 647	26 953	225 260	344 454	19 831	1 655	20 687
	61.1	20	24.3	22.2	18.8	21.7	28.2	25.4	47.6
	12	7.8	7.2	7.2	12.2	15.3	11.9	9	12.4
	8 541 [7]	12 544	7 445	6 779	25 851	47 729	2 398	307	3 672
	0.9	1.3	2.8	3	1.4	1.7	1.5	2.2	2.1

8. Included in B
9. Including non
Sources: Populat
GDP, GFCF,
Indicators of
Wages and pr
Foreign trade:
Total official

	Italy	Japan	Luxembourg	Netherlands	New Zealand	Norway	Portugal
	57 114	123 920	390	15 070	3 406	4 262	9 814
	190	328	150	369	13	13	106
	0.1	0.5	0.6	0.6	0.8	0.4	0
	21 410	63 690	162	6 444	1 451	1 973	4 607
	8.5	6.7	3.7	4.5	10.8	5.9	17.3
	32.3	34.4	31.5	25.5	23.5	23.7	33.9
	59.2	58.9	64.8	69.9	65.7	70.4	48.7
	1 149.9	3 346.4	9.3	289.8	42.2	105.9	68.6
	19 900	27 005	24 186	19 232	12 400	24 853	6 991
	974.6	2 349.2	8.1	248	46.6	71.6	90.1
	16 866	18 957	20 904	16 453	13 675	16 804	9 180
	2.7	4.8	4.3	2.9	-0.2	1.1	4.2
	19.8	31.7	29	20.5	16.4	18.5	26
	9.4	13.1	12.4	10	9.9 (90)	11.7 (87)	7.6
	5.3	5.5	5.5	4.7	4.8 (90)	2.1	4.5 (9
	4.1	8.5	9.9	2.5	-1.3	-6.6	8.7
	18.6	35.1	59.4	24.7	15	23.6	25.4
	17.5	9.2	17.1	14.4	16.6	21.5	17.8
)	49.4	25.4	45 (86)	54.8	..	52.9	39.3 (
)	43	34.4	52.9 (86)	54.6	..	55.3	37.6 (
	0.29	0.33	0.42	0.87	0.24	1.1	0.31
	10 418	10 738	11 973	9 807	8 771	8 558	5 810
	478	282	470	356 (89)	440	378	260
	555	421	413	462	430	502	263
	423	610	252	485	372	423	176
	1.3	1.6	2.1	2.5	1.9	3.1	2.8
	8.3	4.6	9.2	6.5	8.3	7	10.8
	7.1	4.1	..	2.2	5.2	7.6	..
	5.7	1.9	2.3	1.5	7.2	5.5	11.3
	170 258	286 314	8	131 361	9 515	33 808	16 338
	14.8	8.6	..	45.3	22.5	31.9	23.8
	11.6	8.5	..	10.6	10.5	13.1	17.4
	181 925	233 814	..	126 158	9 464	27 164	24 874
	15.8	7	..	43.5	22.4	25.6	36.3
	12.8	13.1	..	10.9	6.8	4.6	22.6
	44 232	55 179	..	12 289	2 902	10 777	10 182
	2.9	2.8	..	1.2	3.7	4.8	4.9

elgium.
-residential construction.
on and employment: OECD, *Labour Force Statistics.*
and general government: OECD, *National Accounts,* Vol. 1 and *OECD Economic Outlook,* Historical Statistics.
iving standards: miscellaneous national publications.
ces: OECD, *Main Economic Indicators.*
OECD, *Monthly Foreign Trade Statistics,* series A.
eserves: IMF, *International Financial Statistics.*

	Spain	Sweden	Switzerland	Turkey	United Kingdom	United States
	39 025	8 617	6 792	57 693	57 649	252 160
	77	19	165	74	236	27
	0.3	0.3	0.6	2.3	0.2	0.9
	12 608	4 431	3 560	18 171	25 726	116 877
	10.7	3.2	5.5	46.6	2.2	2.9
	33.1	28.2	34.4	20.3	27.8	25.3
	56.3	68.5	60.1	33.1	70	71.8
	527.6	239.3	230.9	108	1 008.4	5 610.8
	13 519	27 774	33 992	1 872	17 492	22 204
	496.2	145.4	148.3	201.1	899.8	5 610.8
	12 714	16 877	21 832	3 486	15 608	22 204
	4.3	1.6	2.2	4.7	2	1.9
	23.9	19.4	25.6	22.8	16.9	15.4
	7.1					
0)	4.7	6.2	16.9[9]	5.8 (87)	3	3.4
	9.9	3.3	4	3.1	2.8	−0.5
	21	16	31.6	21.2	13.5	15
	16.1	27.2	13.9	22.5	21.7	18.2
0)	35.5 (88)	59.8	32.5	..	39.7	36.7
0)	36.3 (88)	60	34.2	..	38.8	32.5
	0.22	0.88	0.37	..	0.32	0.2
	7 935	8 994	12 607	1995	9 912	14 891
	307	418	441	29	361	568
	323	681	905	151	434	509
	389	471	406	174	434	814
	3.9	2.9	3	0.9	1.4	2.3
	7.8	6.1	6.2	56.5	7.4	8.9
	7.6	7.7	..	..	8.6	2.8
	5.9	7.2	3.5	60.3	6.4	4.4
	55 353	57 422	63 893	13 057	184 087	393 812
	10.5	24	27.7	12.1	18.3	7
	17.1	8.1	10.2	12.9	11.5	13.2
	87 449	54 659	69 863	22 566	222 522	494 842
	16.6	22.8	30.3	20.9	22.1	8.8
	21.6	8.8	10	13.5	10.7	6
	36 008	12 644	20 541	4 252	25 201	50 791
	4.9	2.8	3.5	2.3	1.4	1.2

January, 1994

EMPLOYMENT OPPORTUNITIES

Economics Department, OECD

The Economics Department of the OECD offers challenging and rewarding opportunities to economists interested in applied policy analysis in an international environment. The Department's concerns extend across the entire field of economic policy analysis, both macro-economic and micro-economic. Its main task is to provide, for discussion by committees of senior officials from Member countries, documents and papers dealing with current policy concerns. Within this programme of work, three major responsibilities are:

- to prepare regular surveys of the economies of individual Member countries;
- to issue full twice-yearly reviews of the economic situation and prospects of the OECD countries in the context of world economic trends;
- to analyse specific policy issues in a medium-term context for theOECD as a whole, and to a lesser extent for the non-OECD countries.

The documents prepared for these purposes, together with much of the Department's other economic work, appear in published form in the *OECD Economic Outlook, OECD Economic Surveys, OECD Economic Studies* and the Department's *Working Papers* series.

The Department maintains a world econometric model, INTERLINK, which plays an important role in the preparation of the policy analyses and twice-yearly projections. The availability of extensive cross-country data bases and good computer resources facilitates comparative empirical analysis, much of which is incorporated into the model.

The Department is made up of about 75 professional economists from a variety of backgrounds and Member countries. Most projects are carried out by small teams and last from four to eighteen months. Within the Department, ideas and points of view are widely discussed; there is a lively professional interchange, and all professional staff have the opportunity to contribute actively to the programme of work.

Skills the Economics Department is looking for:

a) Solid competence in using the tools of both micro-economic and macro-economic theory to answer policy questions. Experience indicates that this normally requires the equivalent of a PH.D. in economics or substantial relevant professional experience to compensate for a lower degree.

b) Solid knowledge of economic statistics and quantitative methods; this includes how to identify data, estimate structural relationships, apply basic techniques of time series analysis, and test hypotheses. It is essential to be able to interpret results sensibly in an economic policy context.

c) A keen interest in and knowledge of policy issues, economic developments and their political/social contexts.

d) Interest and experience in analysing questions posed by policy-makers and presenting the results to them effectively and judiciously. Thus, work experience in government agencies or policy research institutions is an advantage.

e) The ability to write clearly, effectively, and to the point. The OECD is a bilingual organisation with French and English as the official languages. Candidates must have excellent knowledge of one of these languages, and some knowledge of the other. Knowledge of other languages might also be an advantage for certain posts.

f) For some posts, expertise in a particular area may be important, but a successful candidate is expected to be able to work on a broader range of topics relevant to the work of the Department. Thus, except in rare cases, the Department does not recruit narrow specialists.

g) The Department works on a tight time schedule and strict deadlines. Moreover, much of the work in the Department is carried out in small groups of economists. Thus, the ability to work with other economists from a variety of cultural and professional backgrounds, to supervise junior staff, and to produce work on time is important.

General Information

The salary for recruits depends on educational and professional background. Positions carry a basic salary from FF 262 512 or FF 323 916 for Administrators (economists) and from FF 375 708 for Principal Administrators (senior economists). This may be supplemented by expatriation and/or family allowances, depending on nationality, residence and family situation. Initial appointments are for a fixed term of two to three years.

Vacancies are open to candidates from OECD Member countries. The Organisation seeks to maintain an appropriate balance between female and male staff and among nationals from Member countries.

For further information on employment opportunities in the Economics Department, contact:

Administrative Unit
Economics Department
OECD
2, rue André-Pascal
75775 PARIS CEDEX 16
FRANCE

Applications citing "ECSUR", together with a detailed *curriculum vitae* in English or French, should be sent to the Head of Personnel at the above address.

MAIN SALES OUTLETS OF OECD PUBLICATIONS
PRINCIPAUX POINTS DE VENTE DES PUBLICATIONS DE L'OCDE

ARGENTINA – ARGENTINE
Carlos Hirsch S.R.L.
Galería Güemes, Florida 165, 4° Piso
1333 Buenos Aires Tel. (1) 331.1787 y 331.2391
Telefax: (1) 331.1787

AUSTRALIA – AUSTRALIE
D.A. Information Services
648 Whitehorse Road, P.O.B 163
Mitcham, Victoria 3132 Tel. (03) 873.4411
Telefax: (03) 873.5679

AUSTRIA – AUTRICHE
Gerold & Co.
Graben 31
Wien I Tel. (0222) 533.50.14

BELGIUM – BELGIQUE
Jean De Lannoy
Avenue du Roi 202
B-1060 Bruxelles Tel. (02) 538.51.69/538.08.41
Telefax: (02) 538.08.41

CANADA
Renouf Publishing Company Ltd.
1294 Algoma Road
Ottawa, ON K1B 3W8 Tel. (613) 741.4333
Telefax: (613) 741.5439
Stores:
61 Sparks Street
Ottawa, ON K1P 5R1 Tel. (613) 238.8985
211 Yonge Street
Toronto, ON M5B 1M4 Tel. (416) 363.3171
Telefax: (416)363.59.63
Les Éditions La Liberté Inc.
3020 Chemin Sainte-Foy
Sainte-Foy, PQ G1X 3V6 Tel. (418) 658.3763
Telefax: (418) 658.3763

Federal Publications Inc.
165 University Avenue, Suite 701
Toronto, ON M5H 3B8 Tel. (416) 860.1611
Telefax: (416) 860.1608
Les Publications Fédérales
1185 Université
Montréal, QC H3B 3A7 Tel. (514) 954.1633
Telefax : (514) 954.1635

CHINA – CHINE
China National Publications Import
Export Corporation (CNPIEC)
16 Gongti E. Road, Chaoyang District
P.O. Box 88 or 50
Beijing 100704 PR Tel. (01) 506.6688
Telefax: (01) 506.3101

DENMARK – DANEMARK
Munksgaard Book and Subscription Service
35, Nørre Søgade, P.O. Box 2148
DK-1016 København K Tel. (33) 12.85.70
Telefax: (33) 12.93.87

FINLAND – FINLANDE
Akateeminen Kirjakauppa
Keskuskatu 1, P.O. Box 128
00100 Helsinki
Subscription Services/Agence d'abonnements :
P.O. Box 23
00371 Helsinki Tel. (358 0) 12141
Telefax: (358 0) 121.4450

FRANCE
OECD/OCDE
Mail Orders/Commandes par correspondance:
2, rue André-Pascal
75775 Paris Cedex 16 Tel. (33-1) 45.24.82.00
Telefax: (33-1) 49.10.42.76
Telex: 640048 OCDE

OECD Bookshop/Librairie de l'OCDE :
33, rue Octave-Feuillet
75016 Paris Tel. (33-1) 45.24.81.67
(33-1) 45.24.81.81
Documentation Française
29, quai Voltaire
75007 Paris Tel. 40.15.70.00
Gibert Jeune (Droit-Économie)
6, place Saint-Michel
75006 Paris Tel. 43.25.91.19
Librairie du Commerce International
10, avenue d'Iéna
75016 Paris Tel. 40.73.34.60
Librairie Dunod
Université Paris-Dauphine
Place du Maréchal de Lattre de Tassigny
75016 Paris Tel. (1) 44.05.40.13
Librairie Lavoisier
11, rue Lavoisier
75008 Paris Tel. 42.65.39.95
Librairie L.G.D.J. - Montchrestien
20, rue Soufflot
75005 Paris Tel. 46.33.89.85
Librairie des Sciences Politiques
30, rue Saint-Guillaume
75007 Paris Tel. 45.48.36.02
P.U.F.
49, boulevard Saint-Michel
75005 Paris Tel. 43.25.83.40
Librairie de l'Université
12a, rue Nazareth
13100 Aix-en-Provence Tel. (16) 42.26.18.08
Documentation Française
165, rue Garibaldi
69003 Lyon Tel. (16) 78.63.32.23
Librairie Decitre
29, place Bellecour
69002 Lyon Tel. (16) 72.40.54.54

GERMANY – ALLEMAGNE
OECD Publications and Information Centre
August-Bebel-Allee 6
D-53175 Bonn Tel. (0228) 959.120
Telefax: (0228) 959.12.17

GREECE – GRÈCE
Librairie Kauffmann
Mavrokordatou 9
106 78 Athens Tel. (01) 32.55.321
Telefax: (01) 36.33.967

HONG-KONG
Swindon Book Co. Ltd.
13–15 Lock Road
Kowloon, Hong Kong Tel. 366.80.31
Telefax: 739.49.75

HUNGARY – HONGRIE
Euro Info Service
Margitsziget, Európa Ház
1138 Budapest Tel. (1) 111.62.16
Telefax : (1) 111.60.61

ICELAND – ISLANDE
Mál Mog Menning
Laugavegi 18, Pósthólf 392
121 Reykjavik Tel. 162.35.23

INDIA – INDE
Oxford Book and Stationery Co.
Scindia House
New Delhi 110001 Tel.(11) 331.5896/5308
Telefax: (11) 332.5993
17 Park Street
Calcutta 700016 Tel. 240832

INDONESIA – INDONÉSIE
Pdii-Lipi
P.O. Box 269/JKSMG/88
Jakarta 12790 Tel. 583467
Telex: 62 875

ISRAEL
Praedicta
5 Shatner Street
P.O. Box 34030
Jerusalem 91430 Tel. (2) 52.84.90/1/2
Telefax: (2) 52.84.93
R.O.Y.
P.O. Box 13056
Tel Aviv 61130 Tél. (3) 49.61.08
Telefax (3) 544.60.39

ITALY – ITALIE
Libreria Commissionaria Sansoni
Via Duca di Calabria 1/1
50125 Firenze Tel. (055) 64.54.15
Telefax: (055) 64.12.57
Via Bartolini 29
20155 Milano Tel. (02) 36.50.83
Editrice e Libreria Herder
Piazza Montecitorio 120
00186 Roma Tel. 679.46.28
Telefax: 678.47.51
Libreria Hoepli
Via Hoepli 5
20121 Milano Tel. (02) 86.54.46
Telefax: (02) 805.28.86
Libreria Scientifica
Dott. Lucio de Biasio 'Aeiou'
Via Coronelli, 6
20146 Milano Tel. (02) 48.95.45.52
Telefax: (02) 48.95.45.48

JAPAN – JAPON
OECD Publications and Information Centre
Landic Akasaka Building
2-3-4 Akasaka, Minato-ku
Tokyo 107 Tel. (81.3) 3586.2016
Telefax: (81.3) 3584.7929

KOREA – CORÉE
Kyobo Book Centre Co. Ltd.
P.O. Box 1658, Kwang Hwa Moon
Seoul Tel. 730.78.91
Telefax: 735.00.30

MALAYSIA – MALAISIE
Co-operative Bookshop Ltd.
University of Malaya
P.O. Box 1127, Jalan Pantai Baru
59700 Kuala Lumpur
Malaysia Tel. 756.5000/756.5425
Telefax: 757.3661

MEXICO – MEXIQUE
Revistas y Periodicos Internacionales S.A. de C.V.
Florencia 57 - 1004
Mexico, D.F. 06600 Tel. 207.81.00
Telefax : 208.39.79

NETHERLANDS – PAYS-BAS
SDU Uitgeverij Plantijnstraat
Externe Fondsen
Postbus 20014
2500 EA's-Gravenhage Tel. (070) 37.89.880
Voor bestellingen: Telefax: (070) 34.75.778

**NEW ZEALAND
NOUVELLE-ZÉLANDE**
Legislation Services
P.O. Box 12418
Thorndon, Wellington Tel. (04) 496.5652
Telefax: (04) 496.5698

NORWAY – NORVÈGE
Narvesen Info Center – NIC
Bertrand Narvesens vei 2
P.O. Box 6125 Etterstad
0602 Oslo 6   Tel. (022) 57.33.00
                       Telefax: (022) 68.19.01

PAKISTAN
Mirza Book Agency
65 Shahrah Quaid-E-Azam
Lahore 54000   Tel. (42) 353.601
                       Telefax: (42) 231.730

PHILIPPINE – PHILIPPINES
International Book Center
5th Floor, Filipinas Life Bldg.
Ayala Avenue
Metro Manila   Tel. 81.96.76
                       Telex 23312 RHP PH

PORTUGAL
Livraria Portugal
Rua do Carmo 70-74
Apart. 2681
1200 Lisboa   Tel.: (01) 347.49.82/5
                       Telefax: (01) 347.02.64

SINGAPORE – SINGAPOUR
Gower Asia Pacific Pte Ltd.
Golden Wheel Building
41, Kallang Pudding Road, No. 04-03
Singapore 1334   Tel. 741.5166
                       Telefax: 742.9356

SPAIN – ESPAGNE
Mundi-Prensa Libros S.A.
Castelló 37, Apartado 1223
Madrid 28001   Tel. (91) 431.33.99
                       Telefax: (91) 575.39.98

Libreria Internacional AEDOS
Consejo de Ciento 391
08009 – Barcelona   Tel. (93) 488.30.09
                       Telefax: (93) 487.76.59

Llibreria de la Generalitat
Palau Moja
Rambla dels Estudis, 118
08002 – Barcelona
                (Subscripcions) Tel. (93) 318.80.12
                (Publicacions) Tel. (93) 302.67.23
                       Telefax: (93) 412.18.54

SRI LANKA
Centre for Policy Research
c/o Colombo Agencies Ltd.
No. 300-304, Galle Road
Colombo 3   Tel. (1) 574240, 573551-2
                       Telefax: (1) 575394, 510711

SWEDEN – SUÈDE
Fritzes Information Center
Box 16356
Regeringsgatan 12
106 47 Stockholm   Tel. (08) 690.90.90
                       Telefax: (08) 20.50.21

Subscription Agency/Agence d'abonnements :
Wennergren-Williams Info AB
P.O. Box 1305
171 25 Solna   Tel. (08) 705.97.50
                       Téléfax : (08) 27.00.71

SWITZERLAND – SUISSE
Maditec S.A. (Books and Periodicals - Livres
et périodiques)
Chemin des Palettes 4
Case postale 266
1020 Renens   Tel. (021) 635.08.65
                       Telefax: (021) 635.07.80

Librairie Payot S.A.
4, place Pépinet
CP 3212
1002 Lausanne   Tel. (021) 341.33.48
                       Telefax: (021) 341.33.45

Librairie Unilivres
6, rue de Candolle
1205 Genève   Tel. (022) 320.26.23
                       Telefax: (022) 329.73.18

Subscription Agency/Agence d'abonnements :
Dynapresse Marketing S.A.
38 avenue Vibert
1227 Carouge   Tel.: (022) 308.07.89
                       Telefax : (022) 308.07.99

See also – Voir aussi :
OECD Publications and Information Centre
August-Bebel-Allee 6
D-53175 Bonn (Germany)   Tel. (0228) 959.120
                       Telefax: (0228) 959.12.17

TAIWAN – FORMOSE
Good Faith Worldwide Int'l. Co. Ltd.
9th Floor, No. 118, Sec. 2
Chung Hsiao E. Road
Taipei   Tel. (02) 391.7396/391.7397
                       Telefax: (02) 394.9176

THAILAND – THAÏLANDE
Suksit Siam Co. Ltd.
113, 115 Fuang Nakhon Rd.
Opp. Wat Rajbopith
Bangkok 10200   Tel. (662) 225.9531/2
                       Telefax: (662) 222.5188

TURKEY – TURQUIE
Kültür Yayinlari Is-Türk Ltd. Sti.
Atatürk Bulvari No. 191/Kat 13
Kavaklidere/Ankara   Tel. 428.11.40 Ext. 2458
Dolmabahce Cad. No. 29
Besiktas/İstanbul   Tel. 260.71.88
                       Telex: 43482B

UNITED KINGDOM – ROYAUME-UNI
HMSO
Gen. enquiries   Tel. (071) 873 0011
Postal orders only:
P.O. Box 276, London SW8 5DT
Personal Callers HMSO Bookshop
49 High Holborn, London WC1V 6HB
                       Telefax: (071) 873 8200
Branches at: Belfast, Birmingham, Bristol, Edin-
burgh, Manchester

UNITED STATES – ÉTATS-UNIS
OECD Publications and Information Centre
2001 L Street N.W., Suite 700
Washington, D.C. 20036-4910 Tel. (202) 785.6323
                       Telefax: (202) 785.0350

VENEZUELA
Libreria del Este
Avda F. Miranda 52, Aptdo. 60337
Edificio Galipán
Caracas 106   Tel. 951.1705/951.2307/951.1297
                       Telegram: Libreste Caracas

Subscription to OECD periodicals may also be
placed through main subscription agencies.

Les abonnements aux publications périodiques de
l'OCDE peuvent être souscrits auprès des
principales agences d'abonnement.

Orders and inquiries from countries where Distribu-
tors have not yet been appointed should be sent to:
OECD Publications Service, 2 rue André-Pascal,
75775 Paris Cedex 16, France.

Les commandes provenant de pays où l'OCDE n'a
pas encore désigné de distributeur devraient être
adressées à : OCDE, Service des Publications,
2, rue André-Pascal, 75775 Paris Cedex 16, France.

9-1994

PRINTED IN FRANCE

•

OECD PUBLICATIONS
2 rue André-Pascal
75775 PARIS CEDEX 16
No. 47465
(10 94 01 1) ISBN 92-64-14320-3
ISSN 0376-6438

•